Advanced Praise for

Sweet Spot

"It is an excellent book—one of the best in recent memory about marketing."

> — Fred Smith,
> Chairman and CEO, FedEx

"Arun Sinha has called to attention a new way of thinking that will help businesses move the market. Through his 'sweet spotting' skills and strategies, Sinha provides a fresh perspective on marketing processes that can help organizations think differently about how to optimize and create market opportunities to achieve ongoing success. A definite, must-read for marketers of all levels!"

> — Cammie Dunaway
> CMO, Yahoo!

"Arun Sinha confronts the realities of marketing. The book is packed with contemporary examples. An easy and compelling read."

> — Ram Charan,
> bestselling coauthor of *Execution and Confronting Reality*

"*Sweet Spot* demystifies and simplifies the complexity surrounding marketing and branding. Sinha's personal storytelling, experience, and business examples provide an easy framework for achieving marketing nirvana and creating business advantage."

> — Allan Steinmetz
> CEO, Inward Strategic Consulting, Inc.

"I am in heated agreement with Arun Sinha that success comes to those companies where marketing is central to the business. The question is how to actually make this happen. Arun gives us a thorough examination of what the world's best companies do specifically to maximize their marketing game, and how they get all the pieces of the organization in perfect alignment to hit the 'sweet spot' of success."

> — Shelly Lazarus,
> Chairman and CEO, Ogilvy & Mather Worldwide

SWEET SPOT

How to Maximize Marketing for Business Growth

Arun Sinha

John Wiley & Sons, Inc.

Preface

You already know how it feels. Sometimes you're playing a game—tennis, baseball, golf—and you strike the ball just right. Your body is in the right place. Your timing is good. The ball disappears into the distance or slams into the court's furthest corner right on the line.

You just hit the *sweet spot.*

Watch the pros and they hit the sweet spot almost every time. They have technique and timing. The ball arrows down the fairway or out of the ballpark with an apparent minimum of effort. They make it look easy, even though we all know it isn't.

But the notion of the sweet spot is not the sole preserve of the world of sport.

Think of the business world. It, too, has its sweet spots. In business, a sweet spot is a place, time, or experience in which a company's brands, products and services, finances, leaders, and marketers are in tune and in time with consumer needs, aspirations, and budgets. Everything and everyone is aligned; the company's differentiator is cogent, persuasive, and alluring.

Repeatedly finding these sweet spots is the key to growth in increasingly competitive times. Sweet spot thinking is a new way of thinking for a new century.

To my father, my wife Nandita, my son Rahul,
and my daughter Rohini.
Thank you for believing in me.

Acknowledgments

Writing this book would have never been possible if it was not for my 11-year-old son, Rahul. He started to play chess tournaments every weekend last year and I was usually the designated driver. At these tournaments, held in different schools in various states, the kids play chess and the parents wait for them in the cafeteria. In the halls of these schools during tournaments, I started putting my thoughts together for *Sweet Spot*. Thank you, Rahul, for giving me the gift of time to pursue my passion.

This book is a true testament to the "flat world." I live and work in Stamford, Connecticut, the writers are based in London, England, and work with their researcher in Kentucky, and I bounce ideas off a friend in New Delhi, India.

Enormous thanks to the team that worked on this book: Stuart Crainer and Des Dearlove of Suntop Media are the finest writers I've ever met. I'm especially taken by their down-to-earth approach, dry sense of humor, and intellect that challenged me with all my marketing assumptions.

I would have not met Stuart or Des had it not been for James Tate and Michael Pitts. Early on, James sought me out and encouraged me to write a book. On many trips to London, he persuaded me that my story is worth telling. He also assured me that the time required in writing a book is manageable. Thank you, James for pushing me to the next level.

I've been very fortunate to work with brilliant editors at John Wiley & Sons. From the very beginning, Matthew Holt believed in my dreams and encouraged me to give some shape to it. He has been with me every step of the way. I'm amazed at the speed of Shannon Vargo, who can read most of the manuscript in a day and yet has enough energy to comment on it with great suggestions.

Throughout my career I have been fortunate enough to work alongside some remarkable people. It is impossible to acknowledge everyone so to all the people I have worked with and learned from I say a profound thank you.

Some who have showed me the way and still do so on a regular basis deserve extra special mention.

First, I'd like to thank Mike Critelli for being such a great coach. Mike has the highest level of intellectual integrity I have ever encountered and inspires me with his tenacity to achieve even more at every stage. And no one can compete with Mike's rock solid memory. Thank you for giving me a chance to build marketing and a new brand culture at Pitney Bowes.

To Shelly Lazarus, thank you for your support in creating a new brand at Pitney Bowes. You have always inspired me with your simple assessment of situations and solutions. Even though we provide a relatively small amount of business to Ogilvy, thank you for taking an interest—so much so that we consider you as the *de facto* account executive. And the team, Peter Denunzio, Todd Heyman, and others have been great partners.

To Satish Korde, thank you for being a long-time friend and always providing a logical approach on how to manage things during times of mental conflict. I'm inspired by your humility.

To Matt Kissner, thank you for taking interest in me and paving the way for me to be successful at Pitney Bowes and for being a great adviser. I admire your genuineness and down-to-earth approach.

No business could find a sweet spot without great people. Murray Martin, thank you for asking keen questions and instilling the desire to go to the next level. Bruce Nolop, thank you for your advice on organizational astuteness and what's important for the company. Johnna Torsone, thank you for your consistent advice on how to make Pitney Bowes an even better company. Lisa Debois, thank you for being a friend who I can bounce off ideas in marketing. You are a great marketer.

And to Matt Broder, Christine Donahue, Chris Emmons, Kit Hamilton, Sam Kingsley, Lenore O'Connor, Patti Picoli, Matt Sawyer, and the rest of the marketing team—the people who actually made everything happen and made me successful: Thank you.

Bob Mikulay and Mike Mahan, thank you for taking a chance on a young man and allowing me to build Basic brand.

Dinny Devitre, thank you for encouraging me to write a practitioner's book and for constant advice on how to survive in corporate America.

I learned a lot from my friend Allan Steinmetz. Allan has been tremendously supportive over the years. John Sanders and Bill Power helped me to learn the ways of an agency. I'm especially grateful to Chuck Riley who was my manager for many years and stood up for me on many occasions and urged clients as well as others at this agency to accept diversity. Somewhere in heaven, I'm convinced, Chuck is still fighting for diverse ideas and people. Go get 'em, Chuck!

I would especially like to thank the late Prime Minister of India, Indira Gandhi and H. Y. Sharada Prasad for believing in me. Without your support, I would not have been able to fulfill even the smallest part of my American dream.

Gershon Kekst, Wendy Kopsick, and Micheline Tang, thank you for encouragement on writing this book and your consistent advice on Pitney Bowes.

Ram Charan, thank you for your keen questions and helping me sharpen my sweet spot arguments.

As a marketer, I'm constantly learning from my children. They have kept me "in the know" on the world out there with their multiple technology usage. My 11-year-old son challenges my ability to explain things in a simplified way by asking me intricate marketing questions. My 7-year-old daughter would not be left behind with her competitive questions. She has taught me compassion, the gift of innocence, and I dare not go shopping with her. At this age, she already is a strong consumer—knows exactly what to buy and wear.

I thank my parents for instilling the drive to achieve something big. Above all, I want to thank my mother and father who always believed in my dreams and encouraged me to reach even higher by making so many sacrifices for me.

Thank you, Ujjwal my brother, for giving me constructive feedback on the book. I'm sure that Microsoft is lucky to have you in their marketing group, you are the smartest person I know.

At the top of my list is my wife and partner, Nandita. During our 14 years together, she has supported me, prodded me, and encouraged me to grow as a person and professional. Without her support, I would not have been able to devote time on evenings and weekends writing different chapters of the book. She even decided to take a trip to India to visit her family so that I could complete the book without any interruptions.

Finally, I have to thank you for trusting me enough to read this book, a book about my journey that will hopefully help you on yours. Sweet dreams.

Contents

PART ONE

*Marketing needs to change. To get a sense of marketing the way it
should be, you need to understand how companies get into the sweet
spots of the business world.*

PART TWO

*How do you get into a sweet spot? You develop the right skills,
marketing skills. You have to mine minds, demarcate demand,
turn your logo into an icon, mobilize champions-in-chief, and
employ advocates—not workers.*

CONTENTS

Introduction

Over the course of my career, I've had the privilege to observe some exceptional companies. Along the way, I learned a great deal from them, and I also noticed that some of these companies—the very best—do marketing differently. *Sweet Spot* is the story of these exceptional companies—and my own story as well.

Every career is a journey. At times, mine has literally been a journey, one that started in a small town in India and led me to one of America's oldest and best-known companies. At the beginning, I was lucky. I was educated in a good school. This opened doors and helped me break through India's oppressive class system. I started out as a journalist, worked at a variety of publications, and then played a part in the launch of a newspaper, *The Telegraph*, which became one of the largest English language dailies in India.

At this time in the 1980s, India wasn't the economic powerhouse it is fast becoming now. I dreamed of America. No one set on making their American dream a reality heads off straight down a yellow brick road. There are plenty of deviations on the way. I applied and was accepted at Michigan State University, but because of a financial crunch, the Indian government would not grant me permission to exchange Indian rupees for dollars to pay for my tuition. Without a permit from the Reserve Bank of India, there would be no student visa. I tried everything. I wrote letters and even wrote a flattering profile of the regional head of the Reserve Bank of India in *The Telegraph*. But no permit was forthcoming.

Desperate, I wrote to the Prime Minister of India, Indira Gandhi. I asked her and her press secretary for an appointment. Her press secretary, H. Y. Sharada Prasad, was a veteran journalist and a former director of the Indian Institute of Mass Communication, my alma mater. Eventually, I was granted an appointment. With its curved entrance, high ceilings, and wood paneling, the Prime Minister's office in New Delhi was awe inspiring—and intimidating for a 19-year-old. Mustering my courage, I made my case for how I could help the country secure more hard currency by getting my higher education in the United States.

My first "marketing" effort must have been a good one because it worked. The Prime Minister's office decided to intervene and, eventually, I was granted a certificate to get foreign exchange status for my education in the United States.

I arrived in the United States with $730 in my pocket, hopeful about the future and with determination to build something for myself. I dared to dream big. When I graduated from the master's program at Michigan, I got an interview with the advertising agency Young & Rubicam (Y&R). As I was on my way to my first interview at Y&R Detroit on the last day of October in 1984, I heard the news: Indira Gandhi had been assassinated by her own bodyguard. With a heavy heart, I knew that one of the believers in my dream was no longer there. An era had passed, but my dream remained.

Looking back, I was naïve (as are most 20-year-olds). Yet, that naiveté served me well. When I first came to the United States, I was unencumbered with knowledge about how the great American brands were built or how marketing departments functioned. In fact, coming from India, I had to relearn everything I thought I knew about marketing. I now realize I knew very little about business at that time. This meant I started with my eyes wide open. I asked questions. And I am still asking questions. (If you want a book with all the answers, please look elsewhere. After all, the art of marketing is to ask the right questions at the right time of the right people. Instead of answers, I have many suggestions for you to consider.)

Over the intervening years, this constant questioning of marketing wisdom has taken me down some interesting highways and by-ways. A journey that began as a physical relocation from one continent to another, and from one culture to another, became a psychological one. My life has been a journey of ideas and a constant testing of how to implement the best ideas I've encountered. Above all, my life has been a journey of *attitude*. I've tried to develop the best attitude toward marketing, toward customers, and toward business. Through my exposure and management of some of the world's greatest brands, I developed my own ideas about what the role of marketing is in the modern world.

This book evolved from three different kinds of personal energy. First, I was passionate about the state of marketing. I recall reading the observations of Joseph E. Levine, the famed Hollywood producer: "You can fool all the people all the time if the advertising is right and the budget is big enough."[1] That might have been the path to success in years past, but it's flat wrong for the world today. Marketing (and its cousin, advertising) has evolved to the point where it's far more about finding out what the customer wants and representing that point of view inside the company. Marketing should be all about connecting the customer and the company—not hoodwinking anyone, ever! Anyone who believes the opposite (and, regrettably, many still do) irritates and confuses me in equal measure. So I wanted to write a book that defines and models marketing for a new age and a new century.

Second, I wanted to share some of the business world's most inspired moments, strategies, and personalities. I "collect" marketing ideas from all over. Though I work for Pitney Bowes, if I see a great feat of marketing tied to margarine, or automobiles, or package delivery—or any field in the world of business, I always take a few minutes to sit back and relish the moment. Just as all of us admire a sports star who passes, hits, or strikes with awesome beauty, I admire the marketing team that comes up with an unforgettable way to capture the customer's way of seeing things or the customer's attention. When I observe such business prowess, I usually make a mental note, something I can recall just as vividly as a sports enthusiast might savor a legendary touchdown pass in football. So, this book is a testimony of sorts; herein I give many kudos to companies and marketing campaigns that have long been favorites of mine. Along the way, I also pay tribute to some people—my sweet spot heroes, if you will. These are people who have made a difference to the world of business through the way they think about marketing. Most of the time they work, unacknowledged, behind the scenes.

As you'll see, I not only mention these great moments in marketing; but I explain why I think those moments made a critical difference to the companies and the customers who became interconnected by the marketing genius.

As I mentioned before, I have been involved in the marketing world for a long time. I have read most of the great marketing and business books (and met many of the authors). But beyond the reading, I consider myself first and foremost a business practitioner. More influential even than the books have been my own experiences of working with some of the greatest brands. I have been privileged to witness some great marketing moments with my own eyes. And, over a period of years, I came to an epiphany of sorts. That may sound a tad too strong, but I really did startle myself the first time I realized that the best companies—those heralded time and time again in the best books about business practices—*were also* the companies that had exemplary marketing. Could it be, I asked myself one cold winter afternoon in Connecticut, that the best companies of all time were in that elite league *because* they knew something about modern marketing that all the others either didn't know or somehow forgot (or, even, found it impossible to operationalize)?

In time, I started to build the case that companies enjoying enormous, even disproportional, success arrived at that business sweet spot because of the influence and impact of modern marketing—the way it's supposed to be practiced. When my written notes started to fill every file folder and briefcase I owned, it was time to write things down in a more organized way. I poured the energy to communicate my deepest feelings about marketing and today's business world into the pages that became this book. And over time I came to realize that what I thought was going to be a book about marketing was something much wider: It was really a book about business—about the way that business has to change in the twenty-first century. You're holding that book right now, and I can't wait for you to hear what I have to say. This book will bring you new insights and, if translated into practice, new levels of success for your company. Give me a few hours of your time, and I will give you the secrets of the future of every successful business.

Part One is all about what it means to be a sweet spot company. I begin in Chapter 1 by laying out the way marketing has changed the world of business—and how it has changed me. I wanted to give you a bit of a marketing mind-set to understand how the field of marketing has enabled companies—and sometimes blocked companies from finding a sweet spot. In Chapters 2 and 3, I consider what it means to be a sweet spot contender—and what it takes to come through "the qualifying rounds." Sweet spotters move the market, become an alluring investment, outdate to innovate, create a boffo buzz, and court competition. They also exhibit what I call *Z-leadership*. Part One provides you with the rules of the game.

Rules, of course, only get you so far. You also have to understand the spirit of the game. That's why in Chapter 4, I step back a little to view the entire ballpark. The view from the highest skybox is a little different: It is really the big picture. Conclusion? There are two fundamentals that sweet spotters build into their own big pictures: (1) an understanding of the dynamics of corporate growth, and (2) an appreciation of what I call *full-circle marketing*.

Having established the qualification standards and the big picture foundations, Part Two of the book is devoted to making it happen—to just doing it. To repeatedly hit the sweet spot, you need to develop the right skills—marketing skills. To become, or stay, a sweet spot company, you have to mine minds, demarcate demand, maximize your brand, mobilize champions-in-chief, and employ advocates—not workers.

In Chapter 5, we dive into the detail, looking at how the great companies mine minds—how they get into the heads of their customers, their significant others, to truly understand what they want from the relationship.

Deep understanding and respect are good starting points, but sweet spot companies go much further. They know that a profitable business is one that converts customer knowledge and insights into the products and services they will buy. Chapter 6 is all about demarcating demand, reinventing your marketplace to inspire your growth.

Chapter 7 is about moving into the majors. If you want to play with the very best, you have to take your brand and sprinkle something magical on it. You have to transform a workaday brand into a magical emblem. Think Harley-Davidson or Rolex.

The next two chapters are about the folks that make it all happen—that's right, the people who work tirelessly to keep the corporate wheels turning. From the C-suite (so sweet) to the shop floor, in Chapter 8, I look at how you mobilize champions-in-chief. And in Chapter 9, I look at sweet talent spotting—how you hire advocates, not workers.

Finally, in Chapter 10, I put it all together—and hopefully put a whole new attitude into your mind. Those companies who set out to achieve sweet spot status do so with optimism, fervor, and fierce dedication. *Newsweek* reported recently that there are some 35,000 marketing-related books available today.[2] I think you will find *this one* unique. My goal in writing this book was to capture the way companies like Apple, Starbucks, FedEx, and yes, my own corporate home, Pitney Bowes, moved from rough potential to something approaching polished perfection. What these companies did was exceptional. In this book, I have captured their secrets of achieving that same kind of performance for you to use in your own company.

PART ONE

1

Marketing, Sweet Marketing

Some people want it to happen, some wish it would happen, others make it happen.

—Michael Jordan, basketball legend[1]

I'm a marketer at heart and by career. I have always worked hard to become a leader in the marketing of consumer and high-technology products in both the business-to-consumer and business-to-business areas. I love marketing for what it is and what it could be, and I've been blessed to work with high-talent teams to successfully launch 20 new brands in a mix of companies and industries. Some have mushroomed into $1 billion-plus brands. Along the way, I have contributed to growing the brand equity of many world-renowned brands at Philip Morris, Colgate Palmolive, and the Ford Motor Company—as well as Pitney Bowes, where I serve as the chief marketing officer (CMO).

I speak as a marketer who has transformed the Pitney Bowes brand of this $5.5 billion company, garnering top industry honors along the way. I have played a small part orchestrating the huge efforts of many other talented people. Yet, for all the achievements of all of those I've worked with, I look at the marketing world at large and lament at much of what I see and hear.

I am on the road for much of the year talking to our customers, our employees, our competitors, and marketers from an array of other businesses. Their views are as arresting as they are worrying. For far too many companies, marketing is managed the way it traditionally has been. It's as if the marketing function (and the universities that teach marketing fundamentals) somehow missed the millennium and just kept plugging along without recognizing that the world—most certainly the business world—has moved into a new century.

Most importantly, too many in the marketing field today think that their work should be isolated, kept apart from the rest of the company. They believe that marketing *should be* an arcane practice—that marketers are somehow above the rest of the company, ready to save engineering, production, shipping, the rest of the C-suite officers—even the salesforce—when the business horizon is most bleak. Sales collapsing? No winning products in the pipeline? Customers whining on the Internet? Let it all simmer for a few months; then, with trumpets blaring . . . *Never fear! Marketing is here!*

One CMO of a large Fortune 500 company confided to me that he only spoke to his CEO when there was a problem. The rest of the time they co-existed in glorious silence. The CMO couldn't see what the CEO could offer when it came to marketing; the CEO was above such things. It's a mind-set right out of old Saturday-morning cartoon shows, and just as unrealistic. But this attitude is only the first mistake of the traditional marketing minds. Never fear: They're making many others.

It doesn't have to be this way. In essence, that's what this entire book is about: Marketing as we want it, starting with marketing as I now believe it should be defined and practiced.

The Work of Marketing

Let me capture some of my thoughts so you're not left hanging in suspense. Perhaps the most important thing for me to say is that marketing, to my mind, is not static. I meet too many people who think that marketing has become so refined in its tools and techniques that it is the only department in the modern corporation that is supposed to run on automatic pilot. The view of too many is that marketing merely does a few surveys or focus groups and, voila, the next mega product or super brand is born. In truth, marketing is much more work than that. It is the energy center for any company; and, as such, it has to be ferociously engaged with people outside the company (namely: customers) as well as people inside the company.

You heard me right. I did say *inside* the company. Now, most people would agree that marketing needs to be in contact with customers. But I will show you, as we proceed, that being engaged with customers is not simply about demographic polls, surveys, and focus groups. It's about a constant dialogue with the customer to such an extent that the people inside marketing are also inside the heads of those who buy from the business. Yet, though that suggestion will startle many people, I find people are more startled when I propose that marketing needs to be equally in touch with as many employees, as many managers, and as many departments as it can. Your *to connect* list should be as long as your *to do* list.

The most important thing I have learned in my global journey is that marketing must elevate itself to the level of a truly free marketplace. We often use that term, "free marketplace," as a toss-off, something that sounds good in almost any context. But in an age in which customers can buy just about anything they want from vendors large and small located down the street or in another country, the demand on marketing to align the company with the marketplace isn't some nice thing to do. It is a core requirement for doing business in the twenty-first century. I've learned that you can't demote, disregard, or demean the central importance of marketing. It has become the heart of business and, as a result, has to take its deserved seat at the boardroom table. That's why I want to share all that I've learned since I left India. I not only left my homeland, I also left the assumptions that too many still hold about what marketing can do for the success of any enterprise. I've learned what marketing *must* do if any company is to be successful today.

Sweet Sweat

For me, the past five years, in particular, have been fascinating, exhilarating, and at times downright exhausting. Having observed and sometimes worked with some of the great brands, I tried to first identify and then codify what their companies do. But simply trying to figure it out was not enough. For a practitioner, it never can be—not if you want to try to write a book like this. I've always loved that Nike slogan: "Just do it." On the wall of every office I have ever had, I have tacked up a now slightly tired-looking Nike poster with those three inspiring words.

That is what my career and thinking has been driven by: making marketing happen. At Pitney Bowes, I got the chance to take my ideas and put them to the test (more about that later). I am particularly grateful to Mike Critelli, my CEO, for that opportunity. And, did I learn some things. The devil, they say is in the details—and how. My neat theories have been revised along the way. But I am pleased to say the big idea has come through relatively unscathed. It is what I have learned at all the companies I have been lucky enough to work with that really allows me to say for sure that I have discovered a new way of looking at business—one that works. It is a new (and improved) approach to marketing that drives growth. I call it the *sweet spot*, and, in my experience, it boosts revenue and profits. I have seen the results myself.

My notion of the sweet spot isn't a mathematical formula. Success in business cannot be reduced to a neat formula—no matter what a business school professor might tell you. In business, a sweet spot is *a place, time, or experience in which a company's brands, products and services, finances, leaders, and marketers are in tune and in time with consumer needs, aspirations, and budgets.* Everything and everyone is aligned; the company's differentiator from all other companies and competitors is cogent, persuasive, and alluring. Repeatedly finding these sweet spots is the key to growth in increasingly competitive times.

The Sweet Touch

So what is this new approach to business all about? It is based on simple observation. Once you start thinking about sweet spots, you begin to see them all around. But though businesses in a sweet spot may be easy to see, the sweet spot is *not* easy to achieve. Indeed, it doesn't happen often. Sweet spots don't just materialize. Some companies seem to encounter sweet spots and are able to commercially maximize them over and over. Others do not. Though it doesn't happen overnight, some business leaders seem to know exactly what their managers and employees need to focus on *today* so that things happen by a near-term tomorrow. Sweet spots don't happen by accident or good luck. And those who confuse it as such are doomed to fall fast and far behind the competitor possessing its awesome power. Like the tennis player (or any athlete, really) whose prowess is enhanced by a sweet spot—a competitive edge that's an almost mystical mixture of muscle, turf domination, timing, experience, flexibility, resilience, knowhow, attitude, and high-performing equipment—companies that achieve a business sweet spot seem to know their game and play it better than anyone else.

Look around. There are many companies tied to computers. There's only one Apple Computer. Others deliver packages overnight; there's absolutely, positively only one FedEx. Coffee shops go back thousands of years. Then there's the aroma, taste, and smiles you derive every time you walk into the door of a Starbucks, *any* Starbucks. Until mid-2004, anyone searching for news and information online had his or her own favorite search engine. That was before "Googled" hit the Internet world unlike any other word, before or since. Lumber and nails are two of the most basic commodities, but Home Depot has transformed the lumberyard of old into a business that has awakened the dream-it-and-do-it-yourself spirit of more people than anyone could have imagined.

Each of these companies has found "it." They're all businesses enjoying a sweet spot. They have created a business opportunity that was untapped before them. Then they leveraged their marketing so it became the main propellant for their ongoing success. And what they achieved was not points on a score sheet, but maximal business success and as close to a warranty on sustained growth as any company can enjoy in today's marketplace. While some executives of powerful companies might allege that their business was as simple as being in the right place at the right time, sweet spot companies know that it's always been about setting goals higher than anyone else—then developing one's abilities to be able to achieve those goals. So how do they do that? That's the question that I couldn't get out of my head. Indeed, it is the question that should always be in every marketer's head. *How do they do it?*

Others in my field have sensed what I sense about the need to permanently shelve old-way marketing. For example, in 2000, Sergio Zyman wrote *The End of Marketing as We Know It.*[2] Now, Sergio is no wallflower; and when he was chief marketing officer for Coca-Cola, he helped to boost annual sales from 9 to 15 million cases—he knows his stuff. (Sergio even offered me a job with Coca-Cola but that would have meant going back to India and sorting out its business there. Coca-Cola had paid some $65 million for an Indian business, but it hadn't secured the distribution channel. Sergio asked me to sort it out; I chose not to. In the end, because they didn't understand Indian business culture or the marketplace, the company spent the same amount again to buy the distribution channel. And for the record, I still think I made the right decision, but that's another story.) Sergio has been most vocal on how traditional marketing today too often misses the mark and leads companies toward a cliff, if not off of it. Even the best companies (like Coca-Cola) can find itself on the wrong path as a business because its interface with the market hasn't been clearly and convincingly thought through. Christian Sarkar interviewed Sergio on this point, leading to this humorous, if sad, example:

> *There's nothing wrong with innovation . . . [but you'd] be amazed at how many companies confuse what they know how to do, their core competence, with what consumers will buy from them, what I call their core essence. For example, Coke once got into the shrimp farming business—we had core competencies covering purchasing, distribution, sales, logistics, and global operational capabilities. Where it all fell apart was that we never thought about why customers would buy shrimp from us in the first place. Shrimp farming was not a core essence. Consumers simply couldn't make a connection between shrimp and Coke.*[3]

Coke, selling shrimp—like Forrest Gump? Don't laugh at Coca-Cola until you look at your own business history. It's easy in the corporate world (especially using old thinking) to become convinced that if you can do something, all you have to do after that is market it successfully. The takeoffs on two old sayings—*if you build it, marketing will get them to come*, or *success is 1 percent inspiration, the rest is marketing*—were never true. These tired sayings are beyond false; they're vapid. Anymore, such viewpoints will be especially delusional.

Who Needs Marketing?

So, is marketing important? Yes, now more than ever. Most consumer-facing companies know that (although I am staggered by how few business-to-business companies really—and I mean *really*—understand and practice marketing). So what is marketing today all about? "The goal is for companies to better understand customers' buying preferences and link that knowledge to the delivery of products and services that are more relevant to customer needs and to develop closer channel relationships. But the demands on marketing don't stop there," observe Gail McGovern and John Quelch of Harvard Business School. "Companies are looking to chief marketing officers to contain costs in media expenditures, marketing services procurement, and market research. Now that firms have reengineered manufacturing and supply chain processes to cut costs, there is a natural desire to make marketing more effective, too."[4] That's quite a roster of things on the CMO's to-do list.

As I see it, marketing is the essential link between the seller and the buyer. Of course, it's infinitely more complicated than that. And the "new marketing" advocated by Sergio Zyman and many others has not taken hold across any industry I can think of. Those relatively few enterprises that have caught the essence of marketing the way we all would like it to be have indeed enjoyed sweet success. But before we focus on the sweet spots in the business world, let's just review what it is we're trying to get away from and make some quick notes on marketing as we would want it to be.

At a Chief Marketing Organization Roundtable, I gave some thought to the ebb of old marketing and the much-needed flow of new marketing done right. This is by no means a complete list, but it will give you a strong flavor of how marketing was—and is—changing:

Marketing, Old Style	Modern Marketing, New and Definitely Improved
Flock appeal: Consumers are like sheep. They just need to be herded. Presented with the right message, they will automatically buy and keep on buying. Marketing creates and transmits that message.	*Power to the consumer:* Consumers are now empowered. They are able to do things they could not do just a decade ago (e.g., research product choices online). Marketing needs to encourage this trend and make such consumer communication a two-way (and easier) process.
Gullibility rules: Consumers are naïve; if they can be led to believe that they are being told "the truth," they will suck it up. In short, they will believe the message more than they will believe their own senses.	*Smart rules:* Hype and spin may be okay for the political world, but the commercial world has evolved. Consumers are demanding that they be treated as educated buyers, perhaps (probably?) as savvy as the seller.
The salivation solution: Marketing is all about emotion. If you can get the customer to salivate, he will (somehow, some way) find the resources to buy.	*The balance's the thing:* Marketing is an increasingly rational process, one in which the customer's needs (hard realities) must be balanced against his emotions (aspirations).
Wizardry: You can say anything, anytime, to trigger sales. The best way to boost sagging quarterly sales is to turn the problem over to the wizards in marketing.	*Strategy:* Short-term sales goals have to work hand-in-hand with long-term marketing objectives. No one can afford to burn a long-term relationship for a quick sales spike.

(continued)

Marketing, Old Style	Modern Marketing, New and Definitely Improved
Loud hailers: Marketing is a multichannel, multimedia job. Once the message has been tooled, the only other thing for marketing to do is to yell it out from valley floor to mountaintop by employing every available medium.	*Only connect:* Go where your customers are going. Marketing's job is to cut through all the communications clutter and muddy multichannel messaging. Meet your customer halfway; to do that, you have to know (not guess) where she is.
Find them and shake them: Marketing must grab customers by the lapels and shake them awake. All customers are trying to hide.	*Meet and greet:* Marketing has to find out where the customers are and then meet them. The job of marketing is to invite interest from customers who are hoping to be engaged.

You can't help but look at the split between old and new marketing to realize that the gaps are no longer subtle. I like the way Mark Miller, president of Rapp Collins Worldwide, described what he was seeing: "[Old marketing] is based on the simple premise that through mass media I can reach a whole lot of people very, very cheaply." Some prospects will fall off in the initial consideration of the product or service because it doesn't fit into the parameters of their "desired experience." Others, who get past that point, will discover that the commodity is lacking key elements that they consider essential and will turn elsewhere. Still others will be lost when the decision-making process gets down to things like price and color. "The model says if I keep shoveling whole buckets of people into the top part of the funnel, I'll get enough down into my business so that it will be profitable."[5]

How right on is that? The idea of shoveling "whole buckets of people" into the buying pipeline is precisely the single aim and goal of the traditional marketing mind. No wonder the article was headlined *100-Year-Old Marketing Model Is "Cracked."* I would add that it's not only cracked, it's smashed, crumbling, disintegrating, and irretrievably broken.

But you don't have to go back 100 years to see the shifts that are happening in business as registered in the marketing function. Just think about the changes we've seen over the past three decades in marketing and branding strategies. In the 1970s and 1980s, the emphasis was on "whole buckets of people" mass marketing. Pepsi and Nike are two examples of this. Both companies aimed their messages across demographic groups so broadly that it seemed that the challenge was nothing more than "How do we translate the message for *this* nationality?" It was a one-size-fits-all era; the aim being to ship the same products to customers across the globe. Just translate the label. In fact, at the time, it was "cool" to be seen as pushing the same products, the same styles, to an ever-wider phalanx of buyers. Differentiation on the basis of customer segments wasn't that important in the 1980s (although differentiation between brands was). Mass marketing was king. All the marketer had to do was pump out the same message to everyone. And if sales stalled? Simple, turn up the volume!

Then came the 1990s when the emphasis turned to customers rather than masses. In the 1990s, marketing was focused on acquiring new customers and retaining old ones. It was a period of tremendous success for companies like Wal-Mart, the giant superstore chain. Wal-Mart based its proposition on great customer value; and, with stores opening at an ever-faster clip, the chain attracted people from a wide geographic area to their stores. Wal-Mart is now operating in 15 countries with 3,700 U.S. stores and 1,500 elsewhere.[6] But you don't have to patronize an actual Wal-Mart store to know the marketing model it uses.

In our new century, the need to find sweet spots is there and it is growing. A number of trends are converging that make finding sweet spots both more difficult and more essential to business survival. This is an important point—a pivotal point, if you will, so let's just restate that: Sweet spot thinking is about a new way of thinking that meets the challenges of the twenty-first century. In his brilliant book *Good to Great*, Jim Collins (one of my heroes) describes a group of companies that have made the step from good to excellent. I'd like to think that *Sweet Spot* picks up where Collins left off: It offers the modus operandi to become a great company in the context of the new century. So what are these trends that demand a new response?

Jewels in the Crown

The first trend is increasing competition. It doesn't matter which business you are in, competition is increasing and increasingly global. New competitive frontiers are opening up. Look at India and China. A widget maker in Wisconsin now needs to look to Wuhan, China, and Mumbai, India, for the new competition. If you're Dell (market share 18 percent), the company coming up on your outside is the Chinese company Lenovo (market share 8 percent), which is now the world's third-largest personal computing company. More worryingly for Dell, Lenovo has the largest market share in China of any computer company.

As Tom Friedman has said, "The world is flat."[7] It really is. We are all members of the Flat Earth Society now. The advent of digital communication has made it increasingly easy for companies to compete in the world economy. *Chindia*, the vital new combined economic force of China and India, is setting the new agenda. Both China and India are racing to build businesses that can compete directly with Western companies and take business away from them. Their value proposition is very simple: Quality with substantially lower prices. Can you compete?

To give you an idea of what you're up against, through the wonders of web conferencing I attended a board meeting of an Indian company for which I am a director. The previous year's revenues were up 60 percent and a discussion of the year's performance was top of the agenda. I anticipated mutual backslapping. Imagine if your company upped revenues by 60 percent in a year. I was startled when the meeting began. There were recriminations rather than celebrations. The Indian executives were disappointed with 60 percent growth. They wanted to know what had gone wrong. The outcome was that the next year's target was set at more than 100 percent. This isn't wishful thinking. The management team is young and ambitious, they have the strategy figured out, the execution plan is ready, and they are working on building a technology platform superior to any company in the world. They have easy access to capital and are hiring rapidly to grow. The average age of all the employees in the company is less than 30. Their ambition, drive, and optimism are infectious. The meeting ended late, it was 2.00 A.M. where I was in Connecticut; but I felt reinvigorated, as if I was involved with something important. Remember: This is Bangalore, not Silicon Valley.

The company I am involved with is 24x7 Learning, which provides web-based training for thousands of information technology workers in India. The company has the largest market share in the category. The management team is infectiously optimistic and believes that the company can grow by more than 100 percent—perhaps closer to 200 percent—in one year. Yes, I said one year.

As you know, India is now the outsourcing capital of the world. In the past 10 years, the IT services industry has achieved average annual growth of 40 percent. The larger Indian technology companies are growing even more rapidly by providing technology labor to the rest of the world. Tata Consultancy Services is expected to grow to a $10 billion company by 2010; Wipro is anticipating growing to $7 billion by 2009; Infosys Technologies and HCL Technologies are similarly expanding at a rapid pace. To these names can be added Mphasis (as I write this book, a portion of this company has been sold to EDS for $400 million) and Iflex (partly owned by Oracle—thanks to a $900 million investment). There are—and will be—many more.

And it is not just technology. Indian pharmaceutical companies, like Ranbaxy and Dr. Reddy, are competing head-on with global pharma giants and making them rethink their strategies. The Indian auto component and specialty chemical industries are also gaining ground—helped by the staggering fact that more than 400,000 engineers graduate every year from Indian universities.

Speaking with Nandan Nilekani, CEO of Infosys, it becomes very clear that there is no stopping; growth is for good. Nilekani understands the competitive landscape inside out. His goal is to penetrate Fortune 1000 companies and become their partner in every aspect of their business. In some cases, he wants to provide global development centers based in India; in other cases, he wants to provide the engine for growth through product development. Nilekani and Infosys are dedicated to leading technological change.

More is to come. Wipro CEO, Azim Premji, one of the richest men in the world, brims with enthusiasm when you talk to him about the possibilities for Western companies in India. Indeed, companies are now spending heavily in India for the next wave of innovation. They want to be where the action and the innovation is. Vodafone, the British telecom company, paid $1.5 billion for a 10 percent stake in Indian mobile operator Bharti Tele-Ventures, which went public in 2002 on the Bombay Stock Exchange and has seen its market cap jump to $10.5 billion. Kohlberg Kravis Roberts, a private equity firm, paid $900 million to buy 85 percent of software maker Flextronics Software Systems; IBM paid handsomely for acquiring Daksh, a business-process outsourcing firm. Microsoft, Intel, Citigroup, HSBC, and Cisco Systems have all pledged more than $1 billion worth of investment in their Indian subsidiaries to propel innovation for the parent companies. IBM recently held a worldwide investor conference in India and pledged $6 billion of investment to its Indian subsidiary. That's a measure of how seriously Big Blue regards the market; and with good reason.

During the past few years, the Indian economy has grown at more than eight percent per year. Now, it is at an inflection point. Consumer demand is growing three to five times faster than the overall economy. For example, the mobile-phone subscriber base is growing faster than anywhere else in the world and is projected to reach 250 million within five years. Airline traffic has grown from 12 million to 47 million and is projected to grow 20 percent annually over the next five years. With the rise of a middle class in the country, demand for consumer products has grown tremendously.

Indian Starters

The attractions of developing businesses in India are increasingly obvious. Hutchinson Whampoa, LG Electronics, and Samsung have all built more than $1 billion in annual revenue in India. Other companies, such as McDonald's, Pizza Hut, Citibank, Coca-Cola, and Pepsi, are now household names in India.

The successful global companies in India need to have the following characteristics. First, they need to adapt their businesses to local conditions. What works in New York may not work exactly the same in New Delhi. The McAloo Tikki burger, made of potatoes, has the highest sales in McDonald's restaurants in India. Most Indians don't eat beef, so McDonald's decided to respect the sensitivities of the customers and not serve their most popular ingredient in India. Similarly, Pizza Hut's Tandoori Pizza has helped store traffic grow fourfold. Pizza Hut now has more than 150 restaurants in India, and the cash registers are ringing overtime.

The second requirement is to shape the market by introducing approaches that are indigenous to India—but which can then be leveraged in other countries. Colgate Palmolive, Hindustan Lever, and ITC understand this. For example, Hindustan Lever introduced single-use sachets of shampoos and soap products so that lower-income customers have access to premium brands. Sales have been phenomenal. And finally, companies need to have a long-term commitment. One of the biggest mistakes they can make is for the senior executives to make an investment commitment without thinking through the horizon for return on investment.

Choice Rules

Look elsewhere and you will see similarly daunting changes. The rise of India and China is crucial, but there are other issues that their rise highlights:

- *Proliferation of brands:* Think how customer choice rules the marketplace. Today's economy is nothing but choices— 1,500 advertising messages bombard consumers daily.

- *Increasing regulatory change:* The telecommunications, power, and even financial industries have all recently witnessed regulatory change. The rules of the game are constantly being changed and, yet again, competition will increase.

- *No escaping short-term pressures:* At the same time, the pressure is on from Wall Street for results. Senior executives must deliver. If they fail to, they will lose their jobs. CEO turnover is rapidly increasing—research suggests that half of all CEOs are dismissed from office rather than choosing their time to close the office door for the final time.[8] (And CMO turnover is similarly on the rise.) With pressure on companies to deliver improved results every quarter, there is internal pressure. Individual departments must deliver measurable results. They must prove their worth every day of their corporate lives.

- *Mortality:* Given all this, it is little wonder that companies and their brands struggle to stand the test of time. Walk down Main Street in your town and you will see what I mean. Take a look at the store names. Now think back 10 years, 20 years, perhaps even 30 years: How many of the store names were the same? According to the experts, half of all S&P 500 will not be around by the year 2020. The consulting firm McKinsey & Company went back to 1935 and tracked all the Standard & Poor (S&P) 500 companies since then and found out that half of them disappear every 20 years.

And the pace of change is accelerating. It is a sobering thought, but this is the reality of the corporate world in the first decade of the new millennium.

Everything from the emerging threat from Asian companies to over-supply and brand proliferation is putting pressure on corporations and executives. The days when a company could afford to simply make contact with the market—to hit the ball any way that it could—are largely over. Success requires doing it *just right*—hitting home runs (and stealing the bases whenever the opportunity presents itself).

And you know what? If you are a customer, you will be the first to know that you have experienced a sweet spot. And guess what? Once you've had that experience, nothing else will ever live up to it. The reality is that sweet spot companies generate their own loyal customer base—which is one helluva platform for growth. But this warranty for success applies only if you can consistently repeat the experience. You have to hit the sweet spot again and again.

The Meaning of Intimacy

These new realities are already having an impact. For some companies, marketing means more than it did in the past. For them, marketing is neither about mass, nor about customers in bulk: The most successful companies today develop intimate relationships with their customers; today, the *customer relationship* is king. What does this mean? In practice, it means that companies must deliver intimate and powerful customer experiences that build great and profitable relationships. "The most important thing is the customer experience, and how we improve it without commoditizing it," said John Fleming, CMO of Wal-Mart, when I asked him about his priorities.

Businesses must continue to make the customers first in everything they do, from providing them with the best products to offering the most innovative services. Only now, you must go much, much further to reach the sweet spot of sustained success. If I could tag just two signal changes that can help a company move from old-think to new marketing and new management, it would be to:

1. *Initiate meaningful dialogue between your company and the customer.* Ideally, you must invest in developing one-to-one relationships, which can be accomplished through a variety of techniques, including database management, personalized services, and intelligent communications. This also means segmenting your customer base. The rule of 80/20 applies more than ever, that is, 20 percent of your customers provide 80 percent of your profit. Also, you need to communicate with people only in ways that are appropriate to them and only about products and services they are interested in.

2. *You must rethink your operations in terms of your brand.* Everything you do must have a clear brand proposition, something that expresses benefits that are of direct relevance to your customers. You express your brand position through all the marketing mix: be it advertising, direct marketing, Internet presence, public relations, internal marketing, and all other media. (For this concept, I love the term "full-circle marketing." More on that later.) Most importantly, your brand proposition must be understood throughout your organization, from marketing, to sales, to shipping, to service, to finance, to engineering, to after-sales customer service.

So, if you want to find your own sweet spot, then read on. There's no business like a sweet spot business.

CHAPTER

2

Sweet Spotting

Question: How do you deal with the expectations that you will always be the #1 tennis player?

Roger Federer: The expectations will always be high because I want to stay the best and improve constantly.[1]

As with so many things you encounter, new ideas are often easy to understand but hard to apply. As I have thought about the incredible changes sweeping my profession and the companies I have worked for, I have been struck how, in isolated but insistent cases, some companies seem to have found *it*. They seem to have found that incredibly fortuitous intersection of great products being snatched by enthusiastic customers happily willing to pay a decent price for the privilege of doing business with these companies. They're in a sweet spot. How do they do it? Is it just fortune that lands a company in, and keeps it in, the Fortune 500? Or is there something more to this phenomenon?

Then I thought about Tiger Woods, the golfing great who, if not *the* winner in a particular tournament, is usually right up there. Or the incredible consistency of Steve Nash, the Phoenix Suns pro basketball player, who seems to spur his team to competitive status year after year. Could that be why he was the National Basketball Association's Most Valuable Player two years in a row? Or the dazzle that India's batting genius Sachin Tendulkar brings to the game of cricket. Whatever your sport, there are moments when that sport is dominated by one player or one team. In either case, a jaw-dropping juxtaposition occurs: The goals tied to playing that sport better than anyone else and the skills needed to achieve such performance all mesh. And when that happens, the expectations of that sport change. The truly great athletes raise the bar in their sport.

When goals and skills unite in such a fashion, we have an athlete like Swiss-born Roger Federer, who fires a fierce serve and returns volleys with the deftness of his own heroes, Boris Becker and Stefan Edberg. Now, here's a player who has found success and can sustain it for as long as he is physically able. He does not come onto the court for a match without advantage—and it's not because he has a uniquely built racket. The racket is secondary (though it is important—witness Bjorn Borg's forlorn comeback with a wooden racket).

Federer has set a goal to play tennis better than anyone has before him. And he has sharpened the set of skills he needs to make those goals achievable. No matter what racket Federer picks up on any given day, I can assure you it comes with a sweet spot. Why is that? Why is Federer so consistent at being successful? Why don't other players measure up to Federer's standard? Was Federer born to win? Or is it something in his goals and in his training?

What can the business world learn from all this?

Plenty.

How Sweet It Is

As soon as I recognized the stark reality that some athletes are playing with a sweet spot and repeatedly hitting it, I started to look for their corporate counterpoints—Tiger Woods Inc., the Roger Federer of the Fortune 500. I thought it would be an easy list to generate. All it would take is my sense of whether the companies are successful and whether that success was based on the kind of marketing new-think that I now believe essential to sustained success in this new century. But Federer's quote about "being the best" and "improving constantly" nagged at me. Is it just enough to manage with progressive marketing techniques? Is that all that's needed to be designated a sweet spot company? My mental journey is worth noting here because it will help you understand the rigorous set of goals that I ultimately set for companies I consider to be truly sweet spot enterprises.

My process to identify sweet spot companies was semi-academic at best. For that, no apologies. I didn't take the Jim Collins route in *Good to Great* and crunch thousands of numbers to come up with a master list of great companies. My approach was more down-to-earth but, I hope, equally robust. My starting point was my marketer's That's-Truly-Brilliant-Marketing Rolodex (TTBR). Every marketer has one of these—it's a mental list (actually, in my case a bulging file) of companies you have come across doing interesting, successful, and, sometimes, plain wacky things.

Any marketer worth his or her salt is constantly absorbing best practice examples. I have done this over the past 20 years. As I have encountered Truly Brilliant Marketing I have stored it—as a press clipping, a note in my notebook, a request for more information. I often e-mail people I hear about who are doing interesting things to try and get 10 minutes of their time just to hear their unique insights. It's amazing how generous people are with their time and how much you can learn that way.

When I started this book, I spent time looking through this mass of material. All in all there were over 1,000 Truly Brilliant examples I had gathered. Over time, some of these had bitten the corporate dust. Today's notion of brilliance can often fail to stand the test of time. Some ideas had proved less brilliant than they first appeared. Others simply didn't have staying power.

Weeding the Truly Brilliant and Still Useful from the Truly Brilliant But Past Their Use-By Date left me with a much shorter list of companies, many of whom I have long admired. As I looked through the names, my mind was racing. Race with me for a while, will you? There were some 50 companies in my mind. Of these, some were headline names, companies who kept coming into the orbit of my marketing radar.

I'll list these headline companies alphabetically, but that is not how my mind tried to make sense of them at the time, processing pluses and minuses to determine true sweet spot status:

24

Absolut: Here's a company trying to sell hard liquor in a world that, traditionally, has favored beers and wines. But they came back with a range of ways to use their products—and oh, those ads: Absolut Raspberripolitan? Now, here's a company that changed the way everybody looks at vodka.

American Express: They manage financial services very well, and they have also transformed their business numerous times. Now they focus primarily on credit cards, financial services, and travel services. They help business consumers extremely well. They also have developed ways to customize their services to the needs of either small, medium, or large companies. Think of the success of the Bono-inspired RED card concept that donates 1 percent of all your card expenditures to the Global Fund to help fight AIDS, tuberculosis, and malaria. Given this inspirational move, little wonder that American Express is one of the few companies in the world that has been successful in consumer markets as well as working business-to-business.

Apple: Steve Jobs has done it three times: first, when he launched the Apple Macintosh; second, when he launched Pixar; now, he's done it again with super-elegant computing platforms, and, of course, with the launch of the iPod. Apple's philosophy seems to be very straightforward: Find an opportunity for the product, make it extremely easy to use, and serve it up with excellent design and packaging. The company really excels at finding an opportunity—it always looks for a game-changing approach. When Macintosh was launched, they introduced the world to a simple personal computer. When the iPod was launched, they legitimized and legalized selling songs at a nominal cost on the Internet instead of people swapping tunes for free.

British Petroleum: This company was lagging behind the big players like Exxon and Chevron; it was lost in terms of being

#1 in the competitive marketplace. What did they do? They decided to differentiate themselves by introducing a most clever concept: "beyond petroleum." It was all about being more than an oil company, moving into things like solar energy and the like.[2] Brilliant. They even replaced their logo with a sunburst.

Colgate: I remember how Colgate was trailing Crest in 1989. Then Colgate launched the tartar control approach to teeth cleaning, and that started the change of market share. Today, especially after the launch of Total in the late 1990s, Colgate has higher market share than Crest. What a turnaround!

Dell: A lot has been written about Dell, much of it deeply impressive. But what struck me about the company was the way it manages the number of times that it turns over its inventory. Dell's senior management made a commitment to increase the inventory turn—how many times it turns over its warehouse stock—from the industry average of 20, doubling it to 40 in the mid-1990s. The point here is that you can have slimmer margins than your competitors and still make better profits if you turn the inventory quickly. The company started making progress in this area; and, by early 2000, its inventory turns grew to more than 100. This is one of the secrets of Dell's success. What a wonderful integration of the public face and superior internal retooling to make the company's public promises come true.

Disney: The folks at Disney really manage the customer experience—always have! Their philosophy is to start with defining the type of experience they are going to provide the customer and then making sure that all their products, services, entertainment, approach, employee thinking, and management are focused on providing *exactly* that. Sure, there were mergers and acquisitions that stretched their unified vision—and their international expansions did not go as well as they hoped. But, in good or bad times, here's a company that seems to hit the sweet spot over and over.

General Electric: There are a lot of stories about GE, but the real story is whether GE can manage the goal of generating substantial organic growth. CEO Jeffrey Immelt acknowledged that GE hit a figure of 8 percent organic growth in 2005.[3] That's no small feat for an almost $149 billion company. GE did this by starting a new strategy of innovation and strategic marketing. Its former CMO, Beth Comstock, was an inspirational force in making this happen. GE created 80 projects that should generate more than $100 million in business per year; each project had a team to manage the new business. Hundreds of strategic marketers were hired to determine how best these enterprises could solve problems for both old and new GE customers; then GE also hired thousands of salespeople to sell these solutions.

Google: How can one overlook or forget this company? With some touting a future stock price of $500 to $1,000 per share (or higher!), it's amazing to see how those leading Google are interpreting the market signs that tell them where and how to expand. But *BusinessWeek* had it right, despite the ups and downs that have hit Google: With all its "gold," Google will have the enviable challenge of picking and choosing from a whole array of strategic futures. "Google stock, with a price-earnings ratio of 70, represents one of the richest deal making currencies anywhere. That heft has attracted a growing galaxy of entrepreneurs, venture capitalists, and investment bankers, all of whom are orbiting Google in the hopes of selling it something—a new service, a startup company, even a new strategy—anything to get their hands on a little of the Google gold."[4] A nice problem to have. The only question mark I will raise at this point is that, to date, Google has yet to weather a storm. As long as they don't become arrogant, they can weather a storm. A definite risk. The true test comes when the going gets tough. But, simply getting to where it is today is a remarkable story.

IKEA: It has 90,000 employees worldwide and its founder, Ingvar Kamprad, was recently named the fourth richest man in the world.[5] The reports say IKEA is the largest furniture maker in the world (202 stores in 32 countries), yet Kamprad is not content to rest. "Everything we earn we need as a reserve. We have to still develop the IKEA group. We need many billions of Swiss francs to take on China or Russia." Is that a sweet spot mentality or what?

JetBlue: Everyone talks about Southwest Airlines, and there is much to admire there. But in my book JetBlue has topped Southwest to some degree. JetBlue's traffic pattern is focused travel to Florida from the East Coast, and people give it good marks. Then again, if one looks at its stock price over the past few years, it's only worth about a third of its 2003 peak. Is this a down that's soon to be reversed with a wider market share?

Lenovo: Founded in 1984 in a two-room bungalow in Beijing, China, Lenovo now has 4,000 retail stores in China and Asia alone.[6] The 1984 founders? Some Bill Gates kind of entrepreneurs? Guess again. Lenovo was founded by "11 scientists from the Chinese Academy of Sciences."[7] The ownership model is in flux, but the Chinese government still owns about 46 percent of the company. And now the big story: in December 2004; Lenovo laid out $1.75 billion to buy the personal computer business of IBM, which had decided to exit the market and to focus on other business lines. Lenovo also purchased the rights to use IBM's name on Lenovo's newly acquired computer line until 2009.[8] Lenovo, despite those rights, decided to abandon the IBM name to promote its own. After all, with the acquisition, Lenovo became a company with $13 billion in revenues derived from selling computers in 60 countries.[9] Branding gurus were critical. Said Deepak Advani, the chief marketing officer for Lenovo: "But in our industry, there is a tight association between the company and the product, so we have to make sure it is clear that it is really Lenovo selling it to you and not IBM."[10] More global China-based brands will follow.

Nike: Scott Bedbury spent seven years at the company as its worldwide advertising director. During that time, Nike grew to become a $5 billion company. We've all been uttering "Just do it!" for so long that it's amazing how the company, its logo, and this phrase have become embedded into the world's conscience. An iconic company, to be sure.

Pitney Bowes: I'll certainly have more to say about my own organization before the book is complete. Two things I should signal upfront: I think the Pitney Bowes story about reinvigorating an established and highly successful company is a great one, notwithstanding my obvious bias; and, second, it is important to note that Pitney Bowes is making marketing work in the business-to-business world rather than (purportedly) sexy business-to-consumer environment. I must confess that I still encounter many people who think that our work is simply about selling postage—"slapping a stamp on the envelope," if you will. But through a lot of hard work, Pitney Bowes has been reborn. Some 40 percent to 50 percent of our business comes from newly developed and newly acquired software, services, and solutions. What happened to the stamp on the envelope? It's still the core business, but one that has led us into a newly defined marketplace where our sweet spot will shine brightly with customers.

UPS: We could argue that UPS revamped its business and ended up not only broader than before, but in whole new territory: logistics management. It is also going a step further.

For example, they used to pick up Toshiba customers' returned/defective products and send them to the manufacturer's repair center. After they were repaired, UPS would ship them back to the customer. Now, UPS takes a different approach. They still pick up the defective products, but, instead of sending them to the manufacturer's repair center, they are sent to a repair center inside UPS where certified engineers do the repair work. This, to me, is managing the sweet spot in such a way that future growth is inevitable.

It's important to note here that there were dozens of companies on my sweet short list. For weeks on end, my note taking was done at a furious pace. ABB, Amazon.com, Caterpillar, Cummins Engine, ING, LG Electronics, Leapfrog, Mitsubishi, Mittal Steel, Morningstar Financial Services, Petrochina, Procter & Gamble, Rediff.com India, Toyota, VISA, Wal-Mart, Wipro, Yahoo!, the Spanish retailer Zara—companies flew into and out of my mind as I started my search for the links between the best of the best on my marketing Rolodex.

But what would be the standards? I ultimately arrived at six parameters that seemed to be the best embodiment of modern marketing thinking and to have the very best chance of sustained success.

These weren't really goals in the conventional sense. All companies have goals. Management by objective is so embedded in the corporate world that it's hard not to feel that you are accountable for a multiplex of goals running vertically and horizontally through the matrixed organizational world that you and I call our corporate homes.

What I am talking about is bigger than a goal; it transcends all other objectives. It sets the standard for your very existence: your company's collective *raison d'être*, its reason to be. It is the DNA of the sweet spot.

With sweet spot DNA established in my head, I knew I could judge companies more rigorously, more accurately. Here's what evolved. A sweet spot company must commit to doing six things exceedingly well and above all else:

1. *Move the market.* A company might have Exxon-enormous sales volume, but companies have had impressive sales and profits before and slid out of existence in the space of a decade or two. So, it's not the volume of products or services that a company sells that needs to be looked at; it's the propensity for a company to make great numbers and to blitz the marketplace over and over again with products or services that redefine the state of the industry. Remember, the great athletes push out the frontiers of their sport, and redefine what can be achieved. The same applies to sweet spot companies. When a company moves products, it's a business to be reckoned with. When it moves an entire marketplace, it's a company that has started to find its sweet spot.

   Think of what British Petroleum (BP) has done to the petroleum market with its inspired Beyond Petroleum campaign. It is still an oil company, but it has transformed the marketplace and the market's perception of what BP stands for. Instead of being caught in the questioning glare of environmentalists, it has turned the tables and led the charge to reinvent what it stands for and aspires to. Brilliant Petroleum.

2. *Become an alluring investment.* Everyone these days is hypersensitive about not investing in (let alone becoming!) the next Enron. One should not forget—and it's still on the Enron web site—that *Fortune* named Enron "the most innovative company" six years in a row.[11] How many saw that and decided, just because of that award, to invest in Enron? But it's impossible to argue that a sweet spot company is best of the best if, in fact, people might have lost money in it over the recent past (say, three to five years). Thus, it's important to check whether a company has true—preferably organic rather than mergers and acquisitions (M&A) fueled—revenue growth accompanied by expanding market share and a good lift to its publicly traded price to buy a share in its future.

31

3. *Outdate to innovate.* In the sporting world, I am always impressed when I hear that someone on top of their game has decided to make radical changes to become even better. I remember that the Brit golfer Nick Faldo went through a time-consuming rebuilding of his swing. At that time, he was the most successful golfer in Europe. With a remodeled swing, he started winning majors. A company—any company—that dominates the market with a product or service in high demand and then sits back to enjoy the flow of milk from its cash cow is in denial. What such a company is denying is the historical reality of corporate entropy. What is the life expectancy for any corporation? Former Shell executive Arie de Geus researched it in some depth and came up with 40 to 50 years.[12]

Think of the McKinsey research that forecast that half of all companies that are in Standard & Poor's 500 today will be gone by the year 2020, and the other half will be seriously struggling. It's a sobering thought, isn't it? To my mind, the only way to beat that relatively short lifespan is simply to innovate as a way of sustaining growth. But the secret of a sweet spot company is that they not only innovate, they outdate to innovate: They take products or services that have already been successful, and replace them with their own markedly improved version. In this sense, such companies are a sort of virtual monopoly: No one else is doing what they're doing in quite the same way. Which is why competitors never quite seem to catch up with them, try as they might. They command the marketplace the way Roger Federer commands the tennis court.

4. *Create a boffo buzz.* A sweet spot company seems to have more than customers; it has customers who seem to live and breathe for the chance to do business with the company. Think of the way soccer fans swoon over Real Madrid's star player, David Beckham. To be sure, it is not all about soccer, but about the surrounding aura of his persona, his success, his fame, and his brand. When Apple opened its first

store in Japan, there was an unbelievable line of patrons waiting to get into the store. Visit Apple stores on New York's Fifth Avenue or London's Regent Street and the buzz of engaged and interested customers is palpable. When customer satisfaction turns into customer admiration, the press is sure to note it. No buzz is as good as a grassroots buzz, and a sweet spot company seems to have this kind of market propulsion to help it stay on top of its game.

5. *Court competition*. Many companies believe that getting to #1 means that they can and should *suppress* competition. Yet, my own experience tells me that the best companies love the idea of competing. They know that Tiger Woods, unchallenged, would never play to the consistent levels he does; without a competitor, he might as well retire because he'll never play any better. In the corporate world, Microsoft has around 80 percent market share in the operating systems market. Complacent? Not a hope; it creates competition to keep its people energized.

There must be that hungry wannabe nipping at your heels to really fire up the competitive juices. Sweet spot companies use this marketplace ferment to keep their managers and employees focused, to keep the creative juices flowing, to underline the need for constant improvement and unending training. In sum, while I don't know of any company that underwrites its competition per se, the best companies I've studied welcome anyone who can help them rethink their game. Call it "raising the ceiling"—it's an acknowledgment that, in the major leagues, you either get better or get out. And nothing wakes you up to that reality each day more than a hungry competitor. So, if you don't have competition, invent yourself an enemy. After all, if you don't have an enemy, you can't win.

6. *Spark Z-leadership*. I visit many companies each year. If I'm not actually inside the doors of another company, I'm probably on a telecon with one or more of another company's

employees. And let me tell you that there is an intangible feel when I'm breaking ice with a new entity. While this element may be hard to pin down and measure, it's absolutely real. Sweet spot companies have a zest for doing business, an enthusiasm that's so pervasive that it infects the mood of every employee. Please don't mistake what I'm talking about with programs that hand out lapel pins or put mottoes on coffee cups. Any company that I believe is in a sweet spot has leaders who keep the company pumped with the power of their position in the marketplace and their infinite potential for being even better. Leadership is a nice asset for any company to have; sweet spotters have Z-leadership! This is leadership with that extra ingredient, the thing that zings in the atmosphere, the zest for competition. You can't bottle it, but you sure can feel it.

Sweet Spot DNA

For the best companies I've looked at, these six standards have become an unwritten code (in my mind at least) that goes beyond anything that might headline the annual statement of goals and objectives for the company.

A tennis player may be great at serving; another, great at playing the net; yet another, great at backhand plays. But a tennis player who wants to be seen as capable of playing a really sweet game (i.e., to be judged a really world-class player) will be measured on how well he or she achieves all of these things—and more. Similarly, a company is not deemed to be in a sweet spot simply because it does one thing right; in my view, it has to do a number of things right. The corporate graveyard is littered with companies that were great at one aspect of business, but less proficient at others.

Thus, any corporate leader has to keep in mind, constantly, which measures of success will make his company the envy of companies both in and outside its own industry. A company won't even qualify for sweet spot status in the business world unless it understands the basis of what makes up sweet spot DNA. This understanding will open up new vistas of opportunity. In short, sweet spot companies operate very much as Roger Federer put it— they "want to stay the best and improve constantly"—that these six priorities have become part of the corporate *raison d'être;* they have not been reduced to bullet points on a business plan.

Sweet spot companies instinctively know that, without a profound commitment to these overarching goals, they can forget about playing at their respective Wimbledon or Davis Cup championships. Forget these goals for very long and a company might not even get to the qualifying round.

The Qualifying Rounds

Champions aren't made in the gyms. Champions are made from something they have deep inside them—a desire, a dream, a vision.

—Muhammad Ali, boxing champion[1]

"The good news is that marketing is at the nexus of everything," says Dave Scott, vice president of marketing at Intermec.[2] Dave Scott got it right. That's precisely the way I see marketing, a critical function that is too often discounted—no, more exactly, it's marginalized—in its importance to the corporation. I say that with even more passion now that I have written this book. Prior to writing *Sweet Spot*, my view was that marketing played some rather elementary and well-defined roles. Actually, these were well laid out by the American Marketing Association back in 1985:

> *Marketing is the process of planning and executing the conception, pricing, promotion, and distribution of ideas, goods, and services to create exchanges that satisfy individual and organizational objectives.[3]*

This job description only gets you so far. As a result of talking with as many people as possible during the past few years both inside and outside marketing, I have come to believe that the new role for marketing is very much tied to the sweet spot companies I have talked about in the previous chapter. What I found were companies that had goals that few other companies had. In fact, *goals* almost seems incapable of expressing exactly what these companies do. I mused for some time that the better word might be *aspirations*, but here, too, that choice didn't convey all that I am feeling. I have found that a company that is in a true sweet spot is one that *thinks* differently from its competitors and from most companies in other industries.

Of the dozens of companies I looked at, five companies kept coming to the top of any list I drew:

1. Apple Computer
2. FedEx
3. Google
4. Pitney Bowes
5. Starbucks

Now, before you think that I've added Pitney Bowes as a matter of personal bias, I believe, by the standards I am proposing in this book (or by almost any standards, really), that Pitney Bowes is a sweet spot company as surely as Tiger Woods is a talented golfer. Jim Collins thought enough of the Pitney Bowes story to feature it in his book, *Good to Great*. It is also special in the business-to-business world—one that poses its very unique marketing challenges. I could adhere to total modesty and not mention my home company at all, or I can share with you what it felt like on good days as well as bad to be in the midst of a major transformation, the reinvention of a company after a full 86 years of sustained success. Pitney Bowes is the company that it is today because of things that thousands of employees worldwide did. Were my senior colleagues instrumental? You bet. Was I leading the charge? Some days. Many other times, I observed the impressive leadership exhibited by dozens, no—hundreds of others. And to the best of my abilities, I took good notes. So, with your permission, let's press on.

Only Five?

Are there more than these five companies? Absolutely. I could write about dozens of sweet spot companies (remember my Truly Brilliant Marketing Rolodex)—and throughout you will encounter references and stories from other sweet organizations, from JetBlue to Zara. But my purpose in this book is to make you intimately familiar with the sweet spot DNA of how five companies think, then succeed. You'll understand far better what it takes to play in a sweet spot league if I can help you understand what I consider the best of the best.

That brings me back to the sports metaphor that is at the root of this book. It probably won't surprise you that there are many books in print on sports and psychology. At the top of my list is *Sport Psychology: Concepts and Applications* by Richard H. Cox. There is a great chapter on goal perspective.[4] The points made by Professor Cox about the process of setting clear goals are summarized neatly by Donald Liggett:

- It focuses attention on a task. With a goal in mind, the athlete looks more closely at performance and ways to improve.
- It mobilizes the efforts of the athlete. The athlete with a purpose devotes more effort to achieving that purpose.
- It increases the directed persistence of the athlete. The focus and concentration make practice more interesting, and thus distractions are less compelling.
- It promotes examining current strategies and developing new ones. An athlete with a goal in mind looks for effective ways to get to that target.[5]

Shane Murphy, another master of sports psychology, noted in his own book that "for too many coaches and athletes, sport psychology is a mystery, and the relationship between the mind and athletic performance is not well understood."[6] Not so in sweet spot companies; they seem to think it up and make it so. I say this because sweet spot companies really *do* treat goals the way Cox says the best athletes do. They are religious about setting overarching goals for the company. They are focused on their performance, day by day, with a workforce that is motivated in a highly unusual, persistent way to "get it done." Moreover, they are resolute that, should a setback occur, they push harder if they believe they are on course, or they try new things if they need a new course, quickly letting any other distractions fade out of view. Last, they are unsettled if it appears at any time that their strategies aren't going to succeed. Unlike many others, they're not afraid to change strategies if it will help to accomplish their priority goals.

Other companies seem to operate with a subtle uneasiness, worried that they won't have the end-of-year performance numbers that they set 12 months back. Sweet spot companies strike me as uneasy all the time; they behave as if they won't even make the qualifying rounds, let alone get points on the scoreboard. Ask Martin Sorrell, CEO of the world's biggest ad agency, WPP, and he will tell you that keeping people uneasy is part of his job description. The moment people rest on their laurels, empires crumble. The great are restlessly insecure. As Intel's Andy Grove put it, "Only the paranoid survive." Bill Gates observed that the role of the CEO is to worry. If billionaires worry, you better buy some worry beads.

Marketing needs to become the coach that sets those goals and trains the team to execute them flawlessly. *That's the new role for marketing.* The truth is that marketing should make people uncomfortable because it is always trying to push the business forward toward a new horizon. Like a good sports coach, marketing should always be pushing for a bit more—to knock a fraction of a second off the record, or jump a little higher, or improve the athlete's technique. Let's be more specific and look at some of the companies that seem to have the nifty habit of finding themselves in sweet spots. At the end of each company profile, I'll add a few "Sweet Smarts," notes about what you can learn immediately from each sweet spot company.

Apple

Twenty or so years back, I wrote a college paper on the then ongoing battle between Apple and IBM. I visited Apple and found the company and its people inspiring. I confidently predicted Apple would—eventually—emerge victorious. They did, but no one ever thought "eventually" would take quite so long. (Apple wasn't the only beneficiary—I got my first job at Young & Rubicam on the basis of the paper.)

Sweet spot companies offer products or services that possess a special cachet and start a trend. Back in the 1980s, Sony knew what a sweet spot was: They introduced the Walkman that allowed cassette tapes to be inserted into a small unit that attached to your belt or running shorts. You could play tennis while listening to music, if you chose to, because in time Sony introduced shock protection that allowed a continuous playing of music even if the Walkman were jostled. Over a decade or two, Sony's exclusivity wore thin as many other cassette players were introduced by competitors.

Then in 2001 came Apple's iPod. About the size of a cassette, and a tad thicker, Apple's technology was built completely on digitized music. People could take their own songs (or download songs from Apple or many other vendors) and play those songs in their iPod. It was, if anything, even more shock-proof than a cassette player—and the market for take-it-with-you music exploded. Millions of iPods have been sold; in the past year, iPod sales went up 248 percent.[7] Apple is now a $13 billion company; a large part of its sales are tied to digitized music.

But what's significant is that Apple invented not only a product, but a new way of bringing sound into a person's work and play. Lesson one: A great product is one thing, but something that changes people's behavior is many times more powerful. Going back in history, that is why Henry Ford was such a groundbreaking businessman—and a brilliant marketer. While others thought about the mechanics of cars, Henry Ford (himself no mean mechanic) thought of the life-changing potential of cars becoming affordable. Ford saw the potential for cars to change peoples' lives; his competitors saw four tires and an engine.

Apple CEO Steve Jobs, who was tossed out as CEO in 1985, then returned to power in 1997, has always spoken openly about the need for Apple to forget its past and invent a whole new future for itself. He observed that Apple's edge had been, for 10 years or so, its graphical user interface (GUI). It was, for a time, a monopoly. Then Microsoft came out with Windows, and Apple didn't shine as brightly as before. Plus, even with the competitive edge it had (user friendliness via a GUI), Apple wasn't doing all that well four to six years after Jobs returned as CEO.

Jobs had to have said to his troops something like "Forget about it." Whatever he said, they did. Apple forgot about the look, touch, and feel of their older computers and charged into a whole new look—different not only from their own product line but different from anyone else's. It was an enormous risk. One of their chief designers at the time, Jonathan Ive, talked about that risk. As many said at the time, Ive was the "Armani" of the new Apple; and he knew he was taking the company and the marketplace to heights it had never been before. "It's difficult to do something radically new, unless you are at the heart of a company," Ive reflected when Apple launched the wonderful iMac—described by Jobs as "the quintessence of computational coolness."[8]

From the iMac forward, the new look of Apple exploded. Products were produced using a high-gloss translucent plastic and bold colors. Some of Apple's laptops were available in a tangerine motif. And these bold moves don't even count the iPod, which gave Apple a new product line entirely.

To innovate is one thing; outdating to innovate is another notch up. Apple, when it decided to "do something" about making music easier to access and play, could have simply chosen to take the Walkman and make it smaller, lighter, "cooler." But Apple had other things in mind, as Jobs attests:

> *[Comparing] us to Sony is a statement in itself. I'm flattered. We really respect those guys and what they've accomplished over the years. But we're just trying to make great products. We do things where we feel we can make a significant contribution. That's one of my other beliefs. I've always wanted to own and control the primary technology in everything we do. Take audio. For years, the primary*

technology was the [marking mechanism] inside a CD or a DVD player. But we became convinced that software was going to be the primary technology, and we're a pretty good software company.

So we developed iTunes [Apple's music jukebox software that later morphed into the iTunes Music Store]. We're a good hardware company, too, but we're really good at software. So that led us to believe that we had a chance to reinvent the music business, and we did.[9]

It was the decision to move Apple into the digital music business that established Apple as a sweet spot player and as a reborn company. Anytime you can sell four or more million of a product (iPods) in one business quarter, you know you've done something extraordinary. But did Apple stop there? No. It continues to outdate to innovate. For example, a friend of mine has owned about six iPods. Why? Apple keeps making them better, and he keeps buying them. His original iPod was about the size of a thin cassette player. Then came the iPod Shuffle, which allowed people to play hundreds of songs on a device the size of a package of chewing gum. Then iPod Nano appeared: It offered a full-color screen for selecting songs and was half the size of the original iPod. Then, in 2005, Apple brought out what a lot of fans called the "viPod," or video iPod. Smaller than the original unit, the new iPod held more songs, operated faster, and played videos.

Jobs has not always been kind in his remarks about marketers—nor is he reputed to be the easiest person to work with or for. Could that be because, second to him, no one in Apple really speaks for the company in quite the same way? No matter. Apple, with Jobs as the beacon for the company, gets a *boffo buzz* simply because its customers buzz the loudest. Jobs always gives the keynote address at the January meeting of Macworld (which is not sponsored by Apple) in San Francisco. Even if you have a ticket for the keynote speech, some people cannot get in because of limited auditorium space; they have to watch Jobs speak from a room adjacent to the auditorium. And, each year, Jobs uses the occasion to introduce new hardware or software; but what he's really doing is building evangelists.[10] At one time, Apple actually had a "chief evangelist" whose job was to stir up passions in the hearts of customers.[11] Here's a stat: Type "Apple Computer+customers+buzz" into Google sometime; I got over *four million* hits. What's the stat for your company?

Sweet Smarts: Apple

Growth through Your Own Brilliance

Apple is at its best when it is growing and developing organically. Maximizing the innovativeness of its people is the way to go—and the way to grow. Your best bet for future growth lies within your company's walls.

Have You Got a Lab of the Imagination?

Anyone studying Apple should realize that its main marketing force is *the imagination*. Apple believes that business should be about trial-and-error, about exploration, about plunging (not tiptoeing) into new territory. This is why such wild speculation is growing about the influence of Steve Jobs as he becomes more of a player in the world of Walt Disney with Disney's acquisition of Pixar Animation Studios, the movie studio Jobs built in parallel to his work at Apple. But notice the language Peter Burrows and Ronald Grover used in reporting the story for *BusinessWeek:* "The alliance between Jobs and Disney is full of promise. If he can bring to Disney the same kind of industry-shaking, boundary-busting energy that has lifted Apple and Pixar sky-high, he could help the staid company become the leading laboratory for media convergence."[12] Want to be more like Apple? Then give some heavy thought to how to make your own company morc like "a laboratory." But it has to be a lab that delivers what consumers want.

45

Do You Deliver a Great Consumer Experience?

Apple's design is often celebrated. Yes, its products are things of beauty—especially when compared to the grey boxes produced by the competition. But more than that, they have a great user interface. Eighty-year-olds can figure out an iPod. Apple provides a great customer experience.

Are Your Consumers Loyal?

The side effect of this is that consumers become loyal followers. The lines and lines of prospective customers at the opening of the Apple Store in Japan shows how Apple benefits from the buzz created in its customer base.

Are You in Control of Your Place in the Marketplace?

The final element worth noting in the Apple story is its insistence on proprietary control. Apple is as ferocious as any company I know in terms of protecting its proprietary hardware and software. But, consider this: In 2006, Apple started moving to a hardware base using Intel chips. That's right, they are going to start using chips made by the same manufacturer who made technological components for so many other computer companies: Compaq, Dell, and others. Apple has raised the ceiling on itself by doing this. How so? One of the biggest roadblocks in its quest to own ever more market share has been the relatively high price for its products. Sure, it sells an iTune off its Apple Music Store for $0.99. But try to buy one of their laptops, and you'll find that Apple is around double the price of their competitors. The move to Intel technology will give Apple some much-needed pricing parity while leaving them with an even more level playing field. I like this. It's bold. It says that Apple feels it can play against anyone who makes computers, and that's ultimately why it will emerge as a sweet spot business even after it allows other computer makers to match their ultra designs, straightforward approach, and customer friendliness.

FedEx

FedEx is one of the first great stories about a company moving the market. When Federal Express founder Frederick Smith proposed the idea of a company that could ship products around the world even with an overnight deadline, his college professor was skeptical of the idea. Smith went on to establish a $32 billion company that is now a whole network of companies focused on package delivery, office and print services, trade networks, and supply chain services.

FedEx has never lost sight of its popularized corporate motto: "Absolutely, Positively, Overnight." Today, with a transfer hub in Anchorage, Alaska, FedEx can rapidly deliver any of its packages to 90 percent of the industrialized world. That hub cranks packages through a distribution system at the rate of 13,400 per hour.[13] A share of FedEx stock in January 1980 would have cost you $2.77; in 2006, FedEx stock cost over $114.00. Significantly, the stock price has climbed steadily over the past five years. As I write, the company's net income was up 25 percent in the past year, operating income was up 22 percent, operating margins up to 9.3 percent, and revenues up 10 percent to $32.3 billion. This is the mark of a sweet spot company: Its performance is not only reassuring to customers; it is alluring to investors.

Actually, Emery Air Freight was trying to figure out how to move packages more rapidly from one point to another at about the same time Fred Smith was beginning his company. But Smith wasn't just trying to move packages; he was trying to move the market:

> So all FedEx was, a customized system that was designed to solve this problem, to provide transportation capabilities for parts and pieces of the modern age, where you could go from Armonk [New York] to Abilene [Texas] on the same time cycle that you could go from Armonk to Chase Manhattan [Bank] down in lower Manhattan. To do that, you had to have a nationwide

clearinghouse. And it had to be an integrated system where you had trucks and planes in order the give the level of service [that customers needed].

This, truly, was the beginning of the modern hub-and-spoke airline system, only using packages all sent to one location, re-sorted to planes heading to the right destination, and voila: Absolutely, Positively, Overnight. Smith beams that he was, at the time, able to use existing technology to get all this done. The twenty-first-century FedEx is another matter; plainly, what worked for them in the past is not what the company needs for its future.

CIO Rob Carter says that one way FedEx is outdating to innovate is via a system called "Insight." Noting that UPS and others can do something similar but not the same, Carter then celebrates the company's competitive edge: "[W]e took the whole tracking mechanism and turned it around so that as opposed to having to track a package, you say, 'I want to know what's coming to me today.' You can go out there now and see every inbound package, regardless of whether you knew someone was sending it to you."

He then notes how this pays off for customers who are rapidly coming to love the advantages of the new way FedEx does business:

> *In the Northeast there's a company that does bone-marrow-sample testing for bone-marrow transplants. Getting those samples is a very painful process, and the viability of that sample is only about 24 hours. They'd send out kits to collection places, and they never knew exactly how many would be coming in on a given day.*
>
> *Using Insight, very early in the morning they can see every inbound kit that's heading to them and staff appropriately to get every one of those tests done, because the last thing you want to do is run out of hours in a day and have to recontact a potential donor and say, "Do the test again." Because it's not a fun test.[14]*

48

True to sweet spot form, Carter is most complimentary of UPS as a competitor. He tells the story about Insight with the tone of someone who's begging the competition to show how it can be done better—so FedEx can one-up them again.

Is there a boffo buzz for FedEx? The movie, *Castaway*, a 90-minute ad for the company, would suggest there is. From January 2003 to January 2006, you would have doubled your money had you invested in FedEx stock. I know why; now, you do as well.

Sweet Smarts: FedEx

Does Your CEO Understand Marketing?

Talking to Fred Smith, it quickly becomes clear that he not only understands marketing, he respects what it brings to the business. I lunched with him as I was putting this book together and can tell you that he knows marketing inside out. Think of the difference that makes to the way FedEx sees the world and the marketplace. Its CEO is a true believer.

Do Your Customers Trust You?

Anyone studying FedEx for marketing lessons should dwell on the word *trust*. I have little doubt that what FedEx realized early on was that other package deliverers were simply not reliable. I can recall a day not that long ago when I would send something important via courier and wonder when it might arrive and in what kind of condition. Along comes FedEx and its ultra-high level of dependability; that trustworthiness has become the main tool they use to develop a bond between the corporation and its customers. For other companies, the tool might be quality—utterly high and totally consistent. Or perhaps the tool might be user friendliness, making business an easy and pleasant experience. But, as FedEx has taught us all, trust can be built between company and customer because the latter believes that the former will do what they say they will. Absolutely. Positively.

Google

Microsoft is no petty contender, no matter what the contest. And I could have included them in this short list of superior sweet spot companies. So, why didn't I? Well, I find it quite telling that Microsoft, for all its power and prestige, is looking at one "competitor" with the green eyes of envy: Google. Why that is, I'll address in a minute. But Microsoft's envy (or is that fear?) is intriguing, given the fact that Google doesn't even make the kinds of products that Microsoft does. So, what *does* Google do? Few have probably gone to Google, the search engine page, and clicked on the "About Google" link at the bottom of that page. The first sentence of the corporate information page is a mind bender: "Google's mission is to organize the world's information and make it universally accessible and useful."[15] Really? That's *all* you want to do? I shouldn't be cute; the people at Google are serious about their mission.

Larry Page and Sergey Brin are the founders of Google. Two Stanford university students, they assembled $1 million in 1998 to start the now-universal search engine. The fledgling company was just like a lot of hip Silicon Valley start-ups with roller-hockey in the car park, an on-site masseuse, a piano for impromptu singalongs, and a head chef previously employed by the Grateful Dead.

Okay, so Google was, shall we say, normally weird in the beginning. But let's not forget that the waters into which the Google boat was launched were jammed with competing search engines at the time. No one who invested in Google back in 1998 (or, even, in 2004 when it became publicly traded) could possibly have considered it a sure thing. People I knew at the time all had their own favorite tool to find information on the Web. Remember when AltaVista, InfoSeek, Lycos, Webcrawler, and dozens of other engines were competing for dominance? That time is so *past* (because of Google) that Hamline University's 1999 guide to search engines has many page links that have simply expired. News about engines other than Google just isn't valuable data anymore.[16]

How did that happen? How did Google conquer the search engine marketplace to such an extent that it truly dominates, so much so that it now appears foolish to consider investing in any other search service? David Hornick is a venture capitalist whose blog told the story succinctly. "Powerful customer-focused technology with an eye towards making money—that's pretty much the formula. Even brand, which can be prohibitively expensive to develop ahead of customer traction, will likely follow product leadership. Google's success isn't rocket science, it's just good old fashion company building. Good for them for the discipline. It's an excellent model to follow."[17]

I don't want to be guilty of oversimplifying how Google surged into sweet spot status; we'll be talking about Google's standards and practices later in the book. But let's return to Microsoft. Its CEO, Steve Ballmer, has admitted that the company erred mightily by not developing a competing search engine to Google (and to Yahoo! as well). In a report by Allison Linn, Ballmer was quoted as saying that he thinks Microsoft should have done more, sooner, to face the Google challenge.[18] Ballmer added, "We are hardcore about having the best search offering ourselves, with our partners. . . . We'll just keep at it and at it and at it, and I have confidence in our ability to build a loyal user base."

Google has no plans to compete head-to-head with Microsoft's product line. But, the company that Bill Gates built is increasingly finding that its product line is merging ever so subtly into the basic capacity of any computer to log onto the Internet and process information. In short, many believe that it won't be long before there is one mighty application that searches and then processes information in one deft stroke. Again, as Linn reports: "Ballmer said Microsoft's No. 1 research and development priority is to develop ways to deliver software as a service over the Internet, rather than in more traditional ways such as a CD in a retail box." Given that, Google is a direct competitor to Microsoft. This may be the ultimate battle of two sweet spot players.

Sweet Smarts: Google

Your Product Had Better Work

Google's technology works. Its enormous computer system matches—and may yet deliver—its outsized mission and vision.

Are You Inventing the Future—or Is Someone Else in Your Market Inventing It?

Anyone looking at the marketing prowess of Google should underline what it means to *invent the future*. The most significant learning anyone can draw from Google is that the company never considered the present tense market as the place they want to be. Conquering what is successful right now strikes the founders of Google to be precisely the wrong path for the company. In one profile of the company, the founders noted that they would prefer to fund business growth projects "that have a 10 percent chance of earning a billion dollars over the long term." They also boasted: "Do not be surprised if we place smaller bets in areas that seem very speculative or even strange. As the ratio of reward to risk increases, we will accept projects further outside our normal areas, especially when the initial investment is small."[19] Although many corporate leaders talk about the future, Google is a company that teaches that you have to move your budgets, your manpower, and your own mind toward the best scenarios for tomorrow—and this must be done *before* the rest of the company can follow.

Do You Always Absolutely Think of What the Customer Experiences?

Google, like its competitors, employed targeted ads to generate revenue. However, Google made such ads a desired by-product of a search, not an annoying intrusion.

It thought of users. No one wants to be blitzed by annoying ads offering indiscriminate products and services. But ads that appear targeted to your interests are more bearable—and likely to be more successful. None of this is coincidence. Any new product decision at Google has to face a simple but effective filter: Will the new product make things easier for the user or not? The Google wisdom is that the better the user experience, the more easily money will follow. Hurrah!

Is Your Brand a Verb?

Making your brand name synonymous with the activity is marketing nirvana—think Xerox, or FedEx, or Hoover. Americans say they are xeroxing their documents when they copy them; and in Britain, people still talk about hoovering when they use a vacuum cleaner. These examples are local. But googling is a global activity. In what is probably record time, Google became a name and a verb because of its universal appeal. (Apple, too, has added to the popular lexicon by creating its own noun in iPod.) It all started with that almost all-white search page, but it was more than that: The power of the search service actually transformed it into the "official" way to cite online research. Did you notice earlier how I mentioned my web search for Apple by citing Google as my resource? You didn't think about how that made the statistic more compelling. You didn't have to; it was the power of Google's brand.

Can You Make It Last?

The big question for Google is whether it can make its sweet spot last and whether it is capable of discovering new sweet spots as it evolves. The jury is out, but for the moment the company is luxuriating in the sweetest of sweet spots.

Pitney Bowes

I joined Pitney Bowes in 2001 for a fundamental reason: I knew it was a company that had to go through transformation to build on its heritage of success and prosper in the future. Before I joined there was a period of around six months when we met and discussed the issues facing the company that I might be able to help with. During a series of meetings with Mike Critelli, the company's CEO, and Matt Kissner, one of the group presidents, I asked if I would have a free hand to try to change the culture of the company and to get marketing more accepted at the heart of the company. They said not only did I have a free hand, but it was a job requirement: You're *supposed* to do that, they emphasized. The second question I asked was whether I would have a free hand to change all the marketing approaches of Pitney Bowes. Mike's answer was exactly the same. He told me that I was supposed to bring people together and make change-with-a-capital-C happen.

Sweet spot companies have a curious opinion of their own creations. They take their best products, their most popular services, and they work hard to obsolete them by creating even better products and services. In short, they compete with themselves. Their "personal best" is never tied to the status quo, it's always considered a moving target. Pitney Bowes is best known for postage meters; we have held on to an 80 percent market share of the U.S. postage meter market.

Many companies with over 80 years of corporate history and 80 percent market share might be tempted to sit back and recline on their comfortable laurels. But, like other sweet spot companies, that option was anathema to Pitney Bowes. Mike Critelli is a major force behind the transformation of the company. Today, Mike talks about innovation after innovation. He sees robust growth in a business that helps to move over 500 billion pieces of mail around the world each year. Meters are only a part of the company's future; he talks now about flow of communication, database management, life-event marketing, remote commerce such as online auctions, and capitalizing on worldwide postal reforms that will enable people who want to send mail to have more options.[20]

I'm, of course, intimately aware of what's been happening at Pitney Bowes. It's an exciting story, and I felt the need to claim our own spot as a sweet spot business mainly because we have been trying to walk the talk I have been giving on what makes a company verifiably sweet. The first thing we did was to make the conscious decision (again, that overarching goal) to not only move the company but to move the industry. So, we began an intensive process of talking to customers large and small—and we talked to our employees. At the start of our process, we knew we could be better; but we wanted to register exactly how others saw us, both inside and out. We even spoke to 100 journalists. (And that hurt.)

To our great (but expected) disappointment, we heard that Pitney Bowes was seen mainly as a postage meter company. Our image was frozen in time. Why did that hurt? It distressed us mainly because we felt, at the time, that we were so much more than a company that focused on just postage meters. Our capabilities were so much higher than our image. Beyond that, we felt we could be an even greater presence in the market dealing with all the customers' woes that were tied to information flow. I remember when we first conducted some focus groups among two types of customers, loyal versus nonloyal customers. We wrote down our capabilities on paper and asked the two groups what they thought about the capabilities. The nonloyal group got upset with us: "Why hadn't we told them all the things that the company does?" they demanded. At that point I thought my job was easy: All we needed to do was communicate all the capabilities to the nonloyal groups. Then we went to the loyal group and shared the same list. They got upset at us, too. They said: "We are your best customers. Why haven't you shared all these capabilities with us?" This raised big questions about what to communicate to our customers and prospects. It also made me wonder why they were still our customers if we had failed to share this information with them.

Our depression lifted when we did something that I could recommend you to do as well. We went to our 10 best customers, the ones who knew us, ostensibly, the very best. Guess what? We got much better news than we could have expected, because these customers started to tell us things about ourselves that we honestly had not thought of. For example, the really poignant comment was that "Pitney Bowes is ingenious at uncovering hidden ways to improve communications flow." And "Pitney Bowes is an expert in marrying hardware and software." As you might guess, there's a much longer story here; but it is from this "Aha!" that we started thinking about leveraging this aspect of our work into our growth strategy new products, new solutions, and new communications with the marketplace. We started getting serious about having a shared vision, a common view, about what Pitney Bowes *could be*, up and down and all around the company.

At the same time, we redefined the marketplace and put together a growth strategy that said we do not have 80 percent market share but we have only 2 percent market share. This sent shivers down the halls of Pitney Bowes and all employees. You behave very differently when you have 80 percent market share as opposed to when you have only 2 percent market share. The growth strategy called for modest diversification through organic growth as well as growing through acquisitions into adjacent areas. We've made 64 acquisitions to date. Most of the acquisitions are closely tied to what we are good at and what we do now and we find they grow more quickly once they are connected into our distribution network. They make sense, platform acquisitions that increase the breadth of the company. We also defined the Pitney Bowes brand and started on the path to what I call full-circle marketing (more of that later). We created brand values, brand personality, vision for the company, and asked the top 100 leaders to start the transformation of the company. We started marketing activities through advertising, direct marketing, public relations, investor communication, events marketing, and community relations supported by broad initiatives to bring our sales force and employees on board.

As a result, tremendous positive buzz accrued from this initiative.[21] With all of that, Pitney Bowes added more than one-third of its revenue directly attributable to new strategy; it is becoming an increasingly alluring investment with revenues now at $5.5 billion and still moving up. In 2005, our revenue grew 11 percent and earnings grew close to double digit. We're even seeing some "strong buy" recommendations from analysts, which never hurts. The perception of the company changed more than 56 percent among our customers and our favorability grew to more than 76 percent, higher than any other company in our peer group. I will say more about what we did in the rest of this book, but let me just say that there is no greater thrill in the business world than to be inside a company that decides to move the market, become an alluring investment, outdate to innovate, create a boffo buzz, and court competition. A sweet spot experience is something I would wish for everyone reading this book.

Sweet Smarts: Pitney Bowes

Rediscover Your Company's DNA

What you can learn from Pitney Bowes is what I have learned: Sometimes to become a sweet spot player, you have to break the rules about "sticking to your knitting." Anyone remember the famed points from Tom Peters and Bob Waterman's *In Search of Excellence?* Back in 1982, these two legendary authors averred that great companies stick to their knitting, that they recognized what made them excellent and stayed with that formula despite all temptations to move to new horizons. Now, if we inside Pitney Bowes had read that book and nothing else, we could still be the manufacturers of postage meters and postage meters alone. That, after all, was what most people knew us for. That was a major component of our past success. And, we said with humility, no one can make postage meters better than we do.

But as we dug into the real DNA of Pitney Bowes, it was never just about postage meters. I recall the day when I found out that the company had 3,500 patents. (In fact,

Pitney Bowes had more patents than Apple last year.) It was one of the top 200 companies in terms of new patents, and the technology that we invented and enhanced was actually very business-critical. Only a small percentage of our business was tied to postage meters. In fact, postage meters is around 50 percent of our business. We had to realize that our knitting was much more of a quilt than a suit. And as we have explored and exploded that other 50 percent of the business, we have found the path to the sweet spot. So, are you sticking to your knitting to the point of being bound up and tied down?

Starbucks

Sweet spot companies don't rely on their own publicists to tout their achievements. Everyone else can do that. These companies know that if they can go that magical step beyond simple customer satisfaction—all the way to customer zeal—they will attract both the popular and business press and, in turn, become the subject of a buzz built on what others say about the company, not what it says about itself. The first coffee house was established in England in 1652.[22] Starbucks wasn't established until 1971. From the beginning, the company was a special kind of coffee house. According to chairman and chief global strategist, Howard Schultz, "You get more than the finest coffee when you visit a Starbucks—you get great people, first-rate music, and a comfortable and upbeat meeting place." As many have noted, this is what the company calls "the Starbucks experience."[23]

Today, the company reports that even with over 11,500 outlets, it is opening approximately five new stores per day worldwide.

Now, hold on: Isn't this *just* about coffee? What could possibly make a coffee shop company worthy of investor attention? For, indeed, over the last three years, you would have *tripled* your investment had you sunk dollars into Starbucks' stock.

Well, no surprise: The sweet spot path to success is rooted in the goals they set for themselves. It should now be somewhat familiar to you, as I have been driving this message since the start of the chapter. Starbucks became great when it decided:

- *To move the coffee house market:* They would offer stronger brews, better brews, in many combinations—doing so in a climate that was 25 percent chic and 75 percent comfortable.

- *To become an alluring investment:* They knew that, with the right products and ambiance, they could charge more than those shops with 50-cent coffee in chipped mugs. And they did. As profits increased, they sank money back into opening new stores. Then they put Starbucks into Barnes & Noble stores. Then airports. Now, you can find a Starbucks inside stores like Target. Investors applauded.

- *They outdated to innovate:* When *BusinessWeek* named Starbucks its 24th pick for best performing company of 2006, it noted that it was, first, bringing new beverages to their counters while not fearing the risk to their old products (think Marble Mocha Macchiato). They even started selling music. More than that, what BW liked about Starbucks enough to bump them from the 33rd best company in 2005 to a higher rank was the fact that all their old systems could be tossed off to welcome new, better ways of operating. Said *BusinessWeek:* "What's paying the bills is a continued laserlike focus on speeding up transactions, growing abroad, and finding niche markets in the U.S., such as drive-throughs and rural locations. . . ."[24]

- This naturally has led to a buzz about Starbucks that no other coffee shop has. And it might be prudent to make a key point here. You can't be a sweet spot and please everyone at the same time. There are going to be times when products fail when they shouldn't, when service lags when it ought not to. I think it's a signal trait of sweet spot companies that they have a resilience that comes from their customers, not from an advertising campaign.

- Last, Starbucks has courted competition. One could say that there was a fairly low barrier to entry in the coffee shop market. Yet, to be sure: There is only one Starbucks. You can go to Books-A-Million or Borders and find their own version of a Starbucks. I've often wondered if the people who set up these Starbucks wannabes had actually read the Howard Schultz book on how he operates Starbucks, *Pour Your Heart into It*.[25] Starbucks has been *that* open about its principles, employee management practices, and its working spirit. Its web site (starbucks.com) is replete with information about the company's roots and what, exactly, it's trying to do in the marketplace. "Compete with us!" the company seems to say. Many listen. Some try. No one's beaten them yet.

Sweet Smarts: Starbucks

What Do You Stand For?

Anyone seeking to learn from Starbucks should not bury their head in books about coffee plantations, bean roasting, or serving sizes. Starbucks teaches you to believe in the power of ideals. The company is perceived to be socially conscious.

In April of 2005, Starbucks acquired Ethos, the bottled water company founded in 2002 that helps children around the world get clean water. It's a powerfully simple concept. . . . Water for Water. Starbucks and Ethos are committed to raising awareness of the World Water Crisis. Every time someone purchases a bottle of Ethos water the company has pledged to contribute 5 cents toward its target goal of raising at least $10 million over five years.

In the quest to be bigger, better, or both, too many companies take their guiding principles (if they have them) and too easily toss them aside. Starbucks teaches us just the opposite. Don't lose sight of what you care the most about or what you become could be a scary disappointment. Customers will always find it hard to trust you and your company if they sense that you are without an ethical anchor. Right now, can you name the core truths—the embedded ideals—that your company would refuse to abandon under any market conditions or in light of any short-term market opportunity?

So, there you have it, my five sweet spot exemplars. Remember, too, this chapter has been all about the qualifying rounds. These are some of the things you need to do just to get into the big game. As I said before, in sweet spot companies, marketing is like a good sports coach—always pushing for a bit more. It's great to qualify, but winning is a whole different ball game. To do that, you need every tiny edge you can get. Great athletes like great sports teams—are always looking to improve. They practice longer and harder than the rest—that's the external bit. They also have a winner's mentality—that's the internal game. The very best sporting heroes bring the external and internal games together in sweet alignment. That's what makes them great champions. So how does this translate to the business world? It is all to do with *full-circle marketing*. That's what the next chapter is all about.

Growing around in Circles

My job is to give my team a chance to win.

—Nolan Ryan, Baseball All-Star[1]

Let's take a step back. So far, I've advanced the case that companies in sweet spots meet some very high standards and that they achieve such an elite status by setting some daunting goals. Sweet spotters move the market, become an alluring investment, outdate to innovate, create a boffo buzz, court competition, and exude Z-leadership. But there's something more: They don't work with blinders, focusing only on their specific industry, their current competitors. Put another way, sweet spot companies grasp the big picture; this helps them appear even more decisive when they launch a new product or service. Everything they do, they do with *intent*.

Think of it this way: When Tim Gallwey wrote *The Inner Game of Tennis*, he generated an instant (and huge) following. On his web site (www.theinnergame.com), Gallwey comments, "In every human endeavor there are two arenas of engagement: the outer and the inner. The outer game is played on an external arena to overcome external obstacles to reach an external goal." But then he adds, "There is always an inner game being played in your mind no matter what outer game you are playing. How aware you are of this game can make the difference between success and failure in the outer game."

Some sports stars are content to play the outer game. All the time they are winning, they don't give a huge amount of thought to the inner game. If it ain't broke, and all that. But the great champions are always focused on the inner game as well. It is not enough for them to be the best at any given moment. They constantly strive to improve their technique—even if they are already miles (or games) ahead of their nearest rival. Renaldo Nehemiah is the world famous hurdler who broke the 13-second barrier in

1981. He was asked how he stirred up the daily dedication required to become a super achiever. Said Nehemiah, "Hopefully what we see in the sport of athletics—in those who are succeeding and consistently competing—is the result of the dedication, focus, and the internal fortitude that comes from within. What you see is inner personality."[2] Ah, inner personality! That's what clearly identifies the great champions. *It's also what defines sweet spot companies.*

Remember all the hullabaloo about Japanese companies in the early 1980s? At first, folks in the United States put the Japanese success down to cheap labor costs. Then companies such as Honda and Toyota set up factories in America that outperformed U.S. carmakers, using American workers. "Hmmm," said many top auto execs. Building cars, they thought, is building cars. It's got to be the same all over. Then again. . . . *Could it be that these Japanese firms were doing something different?* I've heard at least one investment guru on television say publicly that he no longer recommends any American carmaker. None. He does recommend companies like Toyota, which has grown in market share and profits while the likes of General Motors (GM) and Ford have lost market share and racked up huge losses. My guess is that the Japanese excel at auto making if for no other reason than their commitment to something called *kaizen*, continuous improvement—even if it's 1 percent of 1 percent—they just keep making their cars better. In short, Toyota (another true sweet spot company) is focused as much on the inner game as the outer game. Roger Federer and Toyota are constantly seeking to improve everything they do.

When I worked with Ford, we noticed that Toyota's paint work was always better than Ford's. Why? The simple answer was Total Quality Management. Toyota made its people care by making them responsible for the quality standards on every part of every vehicle. In time, once Ford management picked up on the "secret" to better car painting, Ford's cars improved; but so, too, did Toyota's cars— every model year. Recently, I saw some stats that showed that Toyota employees each generated $85 net income every year; this compared to $9 for each employee at General Motors. Ford was better than

GM; it could boast $10 per employee. That alone may explain why it's hard to find anyone sinking all their pension funds into U.S. automakers. Despite massive total overcapacity in the U.S. car market of 15 percent to 20 percent, the demand for Toyotas continues to grow. The company has overtaken Ford as the world's second largest automotive producer, and Daimler Chrysler as the third largest in North America. The car in front really is a Toyota.

GM's inability to keep up with Toyota is rooted in a series of corresponding failures. Most telling of these is that GM senior management delegated (abdicated?) improvement and capability development to middle managers and supervisors, instead of recognizing it as their core managerial task. GM hasn't had a growth strategy for decades. That explains why, during the course of the writing of this book, I saw that GM lost $1.1 billion in a single quarter and its market cap plummeted to $12 billion—compared with $112 billion for Google and $204 billion for Wal-Mart. In recent years, GM has been simply aiming to keep its market share above 25 percent. Again, it failed. But what kind of benchmark is maintaining the status quo? GM is shaping itself into being the ultimate runner-up. What an honor!

So, does Toyota take enormous solace in all this? Is it time for Toyota workers to take a huge nap? To them, it doesn't matter that GM and Ford are foundering. Toyota (like all sweet spot companies) competes against itself. If you're into NASCAR racing, you know the name Jeff Gordon. He has some 74 career victories; that's a record.[3] Of course, a NASCAR driver is only as good as the car he or she drives *and* the team that maintains that car. And Jeff Gordon knows that. He could be focusing each day, each race on what the other folks are doing, what the other cars have or don't have. He doesn't waste the time. Instead, Gordon is intensely focused on the car he's driving; the race he always wants to win is the race that takes his car to a higher level of performance. Listen to Ray Evernham, his crew chief:

> *Jeff is as good at giving feedback as any computer system you could put on the race car. . . . If he tells you a car is doing a certain thing,*

you can bet a year's salary it is. He doesn't know what's causing the problem or how to fix it. But he does know what a car is doing, and he's on the money all the time.[4]

Think of a great runner who times herself every day—constantly looking for ways to knock a few fractions of a second off her time. She doesn't let up even when she is far quicker than any other athlete. Or think about Tiger Woods, one of the greatest golfers ever. He hit a slump in mid-2006; in fact, he was cut from qualifying for a major tournament. When asked what he would do, he had a one word reply: "Practice."[5] That's the Toyota mind-set, the sweet spot attitude; it's all about constantly seeking improvement.

Like all sweet spot companies, Toyota knows precisely what it is trying to do, in both an internal and external arena. Indeed, it brings them together. Any sweet spot company not only has that "inner personality" but it also keeps a keen eye on the outer arena. They do this by focusing sharply on two things: the reality of business growth and what I call "full-circle marketing."

Growing Your Own

What is the reality of business growth? Here's a solid way of addressing that question: "In an era of unlimited opportunities but constrained resources, the only marketing metric that matters is growth. Driving growth means stretching the traditional boundaries of the marketing function to encompass activities many companies don't even think of as marketing—yet," say consultants Edward Landry, Andrew Tipping, and Jay Kumar.[6]

Growth is the holy grail of business. All sweet spot companies want to grow. They all *need* to grow, and their executives have no doubts that they need to deliver growth. When I discuss growth inside Pitney Bowes, I frame the subject of growth as a choice—and the choice is simpler than anyone might imagine. First, you can continue in the same area and look for incremental growth by growing market share and/or geographical expansion.

Marlboro, one of the organizations whose brand I have worked with, played with its pricing and marketing to achieve this. For many companies, this kind of incremental growth is what's set as a target. Thus, it's on incremental growth that the bulk of marketing energy and budget is invested. Many companies consider it a good day's work if they are spending most of their time fighting over every fraction of a market share point. It is messy and cutthroat to manage toward this kind of growth. But that is how it is inside a great many companies.

Indeed, when I worked with the Basic cigarette brand—part of Philip Morris' brand portfolio and their second largest brand—I would get a phone call from the company president asking if our market share was down by as little as *one-tenth* of a percentage point. In this industry, the statistics come out on Monday morning; so I worked hard calling favors in to get the market share numbers directly from their source late on Friday. That gave me either a weekend free of worry or time to fine-tune my explanations as to what had happened. Either way, I found myself preoccupied with miniscule growth. Not fun.

Route two is through modest diversification. In their book, *Blue Ocean Strategy*,[7] W. Chan Kim and Renée Mauborgne talk of companies moving from red oceans of frenzied competition to blue oceans, a world away from the competition. Actually, the leaps they examine aren't as great as you might think. They cite the example of Cirque du Soleil. If you have watched one of their shows (even on television), you know about the unique combination of music, theatrics, humor, costumes, and (most of all) incredible gymnastics that strike just about everyone as one of the most innovative forms of entertainment anywhere. Innovative? As Kim and Mauborgne observe, Cirque simply took an outdated format—the circus—and redefined it for the modern age. Starbucks did the same thing with the coffee house that was invented in the 1600s.

Modesty is never a great story, and in the corporate world this is equally true. Modest diversification is not a front pager, but it allows a company to move upstream or downstream from their current core. Most growth comes from closer to your core than you might imagine. My belief is that it is this kind of modest diversification that most mature companies should be focusing on. Apple is still in the computer business, but look *how widely* they have defined that turf. Google didn't become a billion-dollar investment by *just* allowing itself to focus on search engines. Get the point?

The final growth option is *complete* diversification. Some companies have done this successfully, but most have failed. Airplane engine makers don't make the best whisky distillers; restaurant operators should best stay out of the machine tool business. It's very hard to abandon one industry and find a sweet spot in another. That's why I seldom allow executives I work with to dream in this direction.

Big Isn't Always Better

The biggest danger in the final two growth-by-diversification options is that the company's execs chase size rather than genuine business growth. "Although any CEO with an imperial instinct can be counted on to trumpet the benefits of scope and scale, my research across more than 20 industries suggests there is little or no correlation between size and profitability," strategy guru Gary Hamel observed. "While a newsworthy deal may temporarily distract shareholders from a company's otherwise lackluster performance, it doesn't do anything to make a company more dynamic, more innovative or more customer-centric. Put simply, you don't get a gazelle by breeding dinosaurs."

Evidence suggests that eye-catching mega-mergers are as likely to destroy shareholder wealth as to create it. A study of 118 mergers and acquisitions found that 70 percent did not create shareholder value. Another study of 160 mergers and acquisitions reported that 88 percent did not accelerate the company's growth appreciably, and 60 percent failed to earn returns greater than the annual cost of capital required to do the deal in the first place.

BusinessWeek looked at 302 mergers and acquisitions and found that 61 percent of the merged companies destroyed shareholder wealth. The mammoth costs of integration, both direct and indirect, frequently exceed the much-anticipated economies. As executives focus their attention on integration, there is a tendency to overlook customers; and market share can suffer as a result.

This isn't to say that mergers and acquisitions are a bad thing. At Pitney Bowes, we have acquired a steady stream of companies in related fields over the past few years. But, mergers and acquisitions have to be *more* than a financial deal. They must be part of a long-term growth strategy. That's why it is encouraging to see companies now making much more imaginative use of partnerships to grow their businesses. Partnerships can serve as the foundations for eventual acquisition, a kind of low-key courtship. Typical of the new partnership culture is Ice Cream Partners, a 50/50 joint venture between Nestlé and Haagen-Daz (itself a subsidiary of Pillsbury). The joint venture brought together Nestlé's three plants in the United States with Haagen-Daz's strength in its home market. Eventually, Nestlé bought Ice Cream Partners for $650 million. Elsewhere, Wal-Mart used an equity alliance with CIFRA to help it crack the Mexican market. The long-term joint venture between the two companies began in 1991 and was expanded in 1992; in 1997, Wal-Mart bought a controlling interest in CIFRA. Partnership preceded acquisition.

Author and venture capitalist Peter S. Cohan has studied successful diversification in the payment services industry that, he believes, offers general lessons for corporate acquirers. "What makes for successful M&A is taking seriously the basic blocking and tackling of diversification strategy," says Cohan. "Our study found that adding sales and profits through acquisitions depends on applying the following management discipline: pinpoint large, rapidly-growing, profitable markets; focus only on such markets where the acquirer's core capabilities—such as operational excellence, marketing, technology-based innovation—will give the acquirer a competitive advantage in the new market; negotiate a reasonably priced deal with a company that offers a beachhead into this new market; and grow market share by integrating the acquired company with care while 'pouring in' the acquirer's core capabilities."[8]

Growth Recipes

Given all this, the lessons that need to be understood about growth are simple:

Understand your growth strategy. The more people who understand and buy into your growth strategy the better. It is amazing how many companies simply don't have a growth strategy. Many others have one, but it is only understood by a coterie of senior execs. Keeping a growth strategy to yourself is self-defeating.

Accept that growth is hard. None of these options is easy. Growth never is. The succession of business books on making strategy work tends to suggest that growth comes sugarcoated: "Simply take a growth pill and growth will surely happen." Not so. There isn't an easy growth strategy—ever, anywhere.

Growth is the leadership agenda. Period. Growth strategies tend to be controversial as, to a greater or lesser extent, they demand change. This is where the role of the leadership comes in to prioritize the actions and develop a growth strategy that can be executed.

Growth is a process. If it is to work, growth is a process rather than a static statement of intent. Think of Formula 1 cars: They run really fast, but they have to make on-course corrections and fuel and change tires. They come into the pits and, after all these things are corrected, the driver is back again on the track. While the driver is taking his laps, the team manager is analyzing every aspect and is ready with the course correction. The development of the growth strategy is somewhat the same. You cannot stop the race to fix the car first; you have to make all these corrections simultaneously.

Growth is the marketer's job. To prove this point, I asked John Fleming, the chief marketing officer of Wal-Mart, about his work right now. His candor revealed that his commitment to growth was both steady and clear. "I'm right now focused on building capabilities, creating a marketing team, and establishing a strategy for Wal-Mart. In the past, we have grown by opening new stores, but this is the first time we are looking at how to make the stores [more] broad and improve the footprint. Where we are focused on is defining the customer segments, identifying the trends, delivering the needs of the customer, and prioritizing resources." Remember which company we are talking about: This is the world's biggest retailer with 1.6 million employees. A staggering 84 percent of all American households shop at Wal-Mart; but take it from John Fleming, there isn't a hint of complacency in its management. It is hungry for growth, because it knows that if it isn't, its sweet spot will evaporate.

Growth is built on understanding. To achieve growth, you must understand the marketplace in great depth. Ask yourself: How big is the market? How far is it removed from our core activity? How much business do we currently have in this area? What is the size and scope of the total opportunity? Then, acknowledge that:

—*You must understand your competitors.* Ask yourself: What are their strengths and weaknesses—as well as our own? What could be our sustained competitive advantage? "It is important to keep people focused on the competition," says Yahoo! CMO, Cammie Dunaway, "especially in a business like ours where every day new competition emerges. The competition keeps you on your toes."

—*You must understand your own core competencies.* Ask yourself: What are we good at? What can we leverage that no one else can provide? Do you really understand your own organizational DNA?

—*You must understand the talent required.* Ask yourself: Do we have the right people, in the right roles with the right skills? Will we have the right people tomorrow?

—*Finally, you must understand the financial commitment your growth strategy requires.* Ask: What do we need to invest to grow?

It is only through asking yourself these questions that you learn what makes your own organization tick and how best you will achieve growth. Self-knowledge is the foundation for growth. Billie Jean King is one of the first women to win the hearts of the general public via her astute tennis playing. She once shared, "I think self-awareness is probably the most important thing towards being a champion."[9] Self-knowledge is the first source of competitive strength.

Growth Champions

"In the end, there's only one measure for great marketing: profitable sales growth," conclude Edward Landry, Andrew Tipping, and Jay Kumar—three Booz Allen Hamilton consultants. Their research identified a small number of organizations—only 9 percent—in which the marketing function was closely aligned with growth. These "growth champions" shared a number of characteristics:

- They can identify their contributions to revenue growth, and they gain added authority from their ability to define return on investment.

- Their members have a broader range of capabilities than their counterparts in other companies.
- They use standardized tools and processes for efficiency.
- They are proactive, not reactive, in providing both guidance and services that they believe add value to the senior leadership team.
- They are perceived by other executives, especially C-suite officers, as contributors to and leaders of the growth agenda.

Every marketer in every organization should test themselves against these criteria.

Going Full Circle

Understanding their growth strategy is common to all of the companies I have cited as having achieved a sweet spot. But this isn't the only big-picture issue they have in common. The second element is that they understand the notion of *full-circle marketing*, something we have worked on extensively at Pitney Bowes. Okay, so sweet spot companies probably don't refer to it by that precise name. But they would still recognize the principle. It is the means by which a growth strategy can be delivered.

Let's go back to basics. I believe there are two fundamental approaches to marketing. In the first, you spend a great deal of money on positioning and advertising. So, for example, you make some bold claims about your product offering or the level of service you offer; and you do this in as public a way as you can. This hammers your stake into the ground and serves as a catalyst to the company. The value proposition, now widespread and very public, becomes an aspiration that the company has to live up to. Senior managers and employees then *have* to deliver the value proposition because you've staked your reputation on these claims. This works sometimes. A lot of companies practice this. But it costs *a lot* of money. Companies spend hundreds of millions (or billions) of dollars to achieve this—witness the marketing budgets of corporate giants such as IBM and Hewlett-Packard. If you market yourself as the leading company for X or Y, then you better step up to the plate—otherwise you'll lose your customers in droves. Nothing is an unappealing as false bragging.

To a significant extent, I believe the preoccupation with multimillion dollar ad budgets and huge marketing campaigns is a confusing distraction. Ad slots in the Super Bowl aren't what modern marketing should be about. They are the highly expensive tip of an iceberg.

Mutual Segmentation

The second approach to marketing is to segment the audience—externally (customers, media, regulators, Wall Street, etc.) and internally (by different functional groups of employees as well as levels of employees). This is *full-circle marketing*—a view of the profession that sees marketing as all-embracing, covering all those inside the organization—and all those outside whom you have targeted as part of a segment that your company would like to attract as customers. The beauty of this approach is that it invariably starts with an accurate picture of a company's internal capabilities and how they might be harnessed to deliver external solutions to potential customers. It asks the questions: Who are we? What are we really good at now—or could become really good at in the future? And, most of all, it forces a company to ask what it can offer to customers. The value proposition follows from that. (See Figure 4.1.)

For the external world, the company then takes this value proposition and creates a brand personality that it delivers through a variety of touch points—such as advertising, direct marketing, public relations, and special events. In addition, the company also focuses on transforming the salesforce, selling *solutions* rather than products or services, improving the efforts of customer-facing employees' efforts, linking investor communications with the brand,

75

FIGURE 4.1 Full-Circle Marketing

and so on. For the internal audience, the aim must always be to create buy-in to the brand values, to create brand ambassadors, with promoting and fulfilling the values of the brand as part of the evaluation of every employee.

Both of these worlds (external and internal) have to work together in unison, meshed with a brand overlay and a focused growth strategy in mind, in order to achieve sweet spot success. If a company can achieve this, they are guaranteed success. And the cost of doing this is seldom more than what companies spend on outdated marketing techniques. In many ways, this is the critical difference between old and new marketing. One is based on the old idea that if we build it (the brand), they (the customers) will come. The other is grounded in a genuine appreciation of what the organization can deliver—its strengths and weaknesses—and an honest dialogue with the marketplace. One relies on dragging the organization into line behind the brand image; the other is all about creating a brand image that accurately reflects the organization's capabilities and its communications commitment. Think about it.

Apple didn't win the following it enjoys among customers by making claims for its products that it couldn't deliver on. Rather, it relies on full-circle marketing to accurately match the company's capabilities—in design, engineering, and customer service—with what its customers want. The brand is the value proposition; and the value proposition is what's special and unique about Apple—now, today, and into the future. With full-circle marketing, internal capabilities and external demand are perfectly aligned. If you get that right, then you have a license to grow. Finding a sweet spot moves from being a long-shot to being a probability.

In full-circle marketing, *alignment is key*. Everything needs to work together.

When the CMO Council interviewed some 400 people on how marketing (and the companies that marketing is part of) could achieve results during periods of increased market competition and volatility, one of their major conclusions was phrased in a memorable way: "In order to truly become a performance-driven organization, it's important that marketers earn buy-in and support from key groups within the business. Integration with sales, IT, finance and other groups is critical to success."[10] In my judgment, that doesn't go far enough for a sweet spot company.

Businesses hit a sweet spot—*a place, time, or experience in which a company's brands, products and services, finances, leaders, and employees are in tune and in time with consumer needs, aspirations, and budgets—only* when (no matter how global, or gigantic, the company) everything and everyone is aligned. Sweet spot companies practice full-circle marketing, which means that *everyone* must become part of the marketing team.

Many marketers think that they are already executing full-circle marketing. Sadly, most are not. Instead, they connect only with the customer through advertising, direct marketing, and other time-tested techniques. What's missing? This halfway-only approach leaves out employees, investors, regulators, and the media. They, too, need to be brought into the circle of marketing if a company is to deliver growth and land in a sweet spot.

Determined to Be Sweet

In Part One, we looked at the notion of the sweet spot, presented some organizations that appear adept at finding sweet spots, identified the sweet standards they meet—and then, we took a moment to reflect on "the big picture" and to consider two key drivers in the quest to find a sweet spot: growth and full-circle marketing. In Part Two, I become much more tactical. I want to teach you all I know about how sweet spot companies *operate*.

Make no mistake: Each of the companies cited heretofore knew they would have to move the marketplace, become an alluring investment, outdate to innovate, create a boffo buzz, and court competition in order to be sweet spot businesses. Achieving any one of these goals would be enough for a sweet spot wannabe. But those really craving sweet spot success know that a piece of pie isn't the whole dessert. Nor is a great serve the whole tennis game.

It's the combination of setting special goals and working on special skills that can make you a sweet spot competitor. The goals you set for your company are external measures of your company's aspirations. The skills you hone are the internal capabilities that will make you capable of achieving your goals.

What did Dave Scott say? "Marketing is at the nexus of everything."

Absolutely right! In Part Two, I will spell out what this means in practice. I'll explain what you can and must do to help your company create a sweeter future for all concerned. Or, to put it another way, I'll tell you what it means—and what it takes—to step up to the plate and take a sweet swing at the ball.

PART TWO

CHAPTER

5

Mining Minds

Sweet Spot Skill #1: Learn to march to the beat of the buyer. To do that, you have to do more than love the customer: you have to think the way he thinks and grow the way she grows.

"I Want It Now" is the title of a song from the *Charlie and the Chocolate Factory* movie made in the 1970s. In the movie, the song was the theme of a precocious, demanding child. Now, we are all singing the same tune: We want it now!

And how. Consumers are demanding. Extraordinarily so. Have you ever worked in a store? Everyone should. People are fickle, fussy, feisty, occasionally plain fearsome, and sometimes fine. But one thing is abundantly clear whether you're working in a one-store-town in Iowa or Macy's in Manhattan: Consumers want a product or service, exactly the way they want it, when they want it, and where they want it. If they want to buy their mom's birthday flowers over the Internet at 3:00 A.M., your bricks-and-mortar florist has to figure out a way to compete.

There is nothing unreasonable in this—although not all marketers see it that way. Why shouldn't consumers get exactly what they want—where, when, and how they want it—when the choices are practically limitless?

And consumers come fully armed. In years gone by, marketers knew more than the consumers—or thought they did. Today's consumers have more information, sometimes more than the manufacturers. Customers arrive at your store having already done a price comparison on the Web. They want to know how your prices compare with the specialist store in Warsaw, Poland, that promises overnight delivery anywhere in the world. Marketers are not necessarily pushing information onto consumers; consumers are pulling information about companies as they need it.

More of Everything

Look at media and entertainment. Today, more than 40,000 books are published each year in the United States. Time Warner Cable offers over 500 television channels in the New York area alone.

In the wireless market, carriers have moved from basic demographic segments to dozens of needs- and value-based segments. The number of discrete offerings has grown into the hundreds. The same is true in pharmaceuticals, automotive, retail banking, and mail and package industries. Even packaged goods companies are experiencing significant growth in segments. Proliferation is happening everywhere to everyone. More. More. More.

So, how do marketers respond to these new realities? We attempt to satisfy consumer needs, wants, and aspirations by giving them more—not just more choices but also more methods of delivery. The channels and touch points through which these offerings are delivered (sales force, channel partners, web, etc.) are more numerous than ever, with customers expecting and demanding freedom to migrate across channels. Multichannels are here to stay.

Companies now solicit interest through one channel—say, direct mail—close the deal through another channel—perhaps the salesforce—deliver it through another channel—the mail—gain additional consumer information via the Internet and elicit feedback by phone. The challenge is as obvious as it is demanding: How do you coordinate all this activity and ensure that the customer gets a consistent experience from each channel?

The number of media vehicles relevant to marketers is proliferating as well. We are all aware of the growth rates in channels such as the Internet, viral marketing, blogs, satellite radio, in-store proprietary networks, and—I can go on forever. This is all creating a highly complex environment for marketers to navigate.

And we know that more is not necessarily better.

There is evidence that as the number of customer touch points grows cost efficiency decreases. According to McKinsey, in the B-to-B world, return on capital gets cut almost in half as the number of discrete touch points doubles.

83

So how do you profit from proliferation? In my experience, you need to do at least these six things with relentless energy:

1. Get inside the consumer's mind.
2. Segment your market *sweetly.*
3. Offer solutions with savvy—and a smile.
4. Hardwire your team to your customers.
5. Communicate consistently, with one voice.
6. Build a relationship.

Get Inside the Consumer's Mind

The starting point of this—and almost everything else—is to get in line with what customers actually want. You can have the best analysis in the world and the most erudite strategy. You can have total C-suite buy-in for that strategy. But none of it is worth a hill of branded beans if you don't understand the customer. In other words, the sweet spot mantra is: Align with customer insights; align, align, align.

Jim Barnes, the author of seven books and principal of the Canadian firm, Barnes Marketing Associates, contends:

> *To understand loyalty, we have to understand the kind of emotional attachment the loyal customer has to the company or brand. It's much more than how often he or she buys from us, or how much he or she spends annually, or what share of his or her wallet we have. These are all behavioral measures. To understand whether customers are truly loyal, we have to understand how they feel toward doing business with us, what role our company or product plays in their lives, and how they would feel if we were no longer available. This requires much deeper insight into customers' lives and how they feel about the companies and brands with which they deal.*[1]

Sweet spot companies don't consider research and development an inside job. Whether it's R&D (or any other corporate department), these companies know that the best market intelligence is rooted in the minds of their current or prospective customers. Customer-centric innovation is the new mantra.

I worked with Ford, and the way they approached innovation was riveting. Developing new cars takes four to six years, so you have to think about what consumers will want in the future. To address this, Ford would look at what was happening in other forward-looking industries—such as furniture design and high-tech companies in Silicon Valley. It would bring people from those industries together to showcase future Ford products to try to get a handle on the features and technology likely to be important to consumers in the next five or so years.

One of the things Ford spotted was that consumers were increasingly eating breakfast away from home. Instead of making coffee, they'd grab coffee on their way to work. This trend was spotted in the 1980s. As a result, Ford cars in the 1990s all had cup holders so that harried commuters could place their morning coffee somewhere safe. A small thing, but completely consumer-centric.

Apple takes enormous pride in how it taps into the minds of its buyers early in the product development cycle. Apple is, in fact, ferocious about getting any and all customer feedback channeled to the product pipeline; and, of course, those developing the products are often out taking the pulse of buyers. The net effect is that the company marches to the beat of the buyer. As CEO Steve Jobs phrases it:

> I get asked a lot why Apple's customers are so loyal. It's not because they belong to the Church of Mac! That's ridiculous. It's because when you buy our products, and three months later you get stuck on something, you quickly figure out [how to get past it]. And you think, "Wow, someone over there at Apple actually thought of this!" And then three months later you try to do something you hadn't tried before, and it works, and you think "Hey, they thought of that, too." And then six months later it happens again. There's almost no product in the world that you have that experience with, but you have it with a Mac. And you have it with an iPod.[2]

Cammie Dunaway, CMO of Yahoo!, sings from the same consumer-driven hymn sheet. She argues that the CMO's role starts from understanding the marketplace and unlocking customer insights to grow the company. "The CMO has to see him or herself as the champion of the consumer. In technology companies, however, you have to be careful that product development and engineering are very closely tied to the consumer as well. So you don't own the consumer; instead there are other functional heads who are the joint owner of the consumer," she told me. "As a CMO you become the spark for customer insights. I consider my role to be the catalyst for consumer issues." As part of this, Cammie ensures that all Yahoo! executives, no matter what their area or seniority, understand the insights gathered from consumers and have the opportunity to strike up relationships with consumers. Among other things, senior executives conduct one-on-one interviews with consumers. Sweet marketing is one-on-one. Always.

Basic Understanding

When it comes to getting into the minds of consumers, I learned a lot at Philip Morris. One experience stands out. It took place on the ninth floor of 120 Park Avenue, the company's world headquarters where there is a conference room commonly referred to as the "fishbowl." All major decisions for the growth of the company are made in this room. People walking in the hallway can see the participants in the conference room.

The day I was there, in the early 1990s, was one of the rare times when the window blinds were closed. No one from outside could see in. I was pacing up and down the hallway waiting for my turn to be called into the room. At that point, I felt that this would be the most important presentation of my life: My success was dependent on the outcome of this meeting. There were nine people in the conference room who controlled more than $24 billion in revenue. But they were all looking at Geoff Bible, the head of the tobacco business worldwide, who would either make my day (or year, I should say) or I'd be going away empty-handed—and worrying about my next job.

Geoff was a very charismatic leader who had a passion for the tobacco industry. He subsequently became known as the leader who believed: "If you are right, you fight." After becoming the chairman of Philip Morris, Geoff fought in the courts for the viability of the tobacco business, but he was also instrumental in settling the landmark tobacco litigation in 1998 with the states' attorneys general in which the tobacco industry agreed to pay $268 billion over 25 years.

I walked into the fishbowl with a map of the United States. I had colored it the night before in three different colors: Green where the market share of the Basic cigarette brand was growing; yellow where the market share was stable; and red where it was declining. I was the brand manager for Basic, a discount brand cheaper than premium brands such as Marlboro, Benson & Hedges, and Virginia Slims.

Basic had experienced extraordinary growth. The brand went from zero to five share points in just one year, racking up more than a billion dollars in sales and $500 million plus in pretax operating profit. But, more importantly, and the point I was desperate to make to the folks in the conference room, Basic was growing without taking any share away from the premium brand Marlboro.

The C-suite of Philip Morris was determined that if a discount brand from its company started cannibalizing the premium brands, they would stop supporting the brand with any marketing dollars. This would have meant slow death for Basic. The colored map not only told the story of where Basic was growing in the United States but also identified the markets where Marlboro was declining. We had run all kinds of statistical analyses to prove that the growth of Basic was not coming from Marlboro. I had also built an analytical model that projected Basic's share, discount category share, and Marlboro's share based on the types of marketing support we were providing. I took the group through a well-rehearsed presentation during which I showed them how Basic had become a strong brand in itself and was attracting very different types of buyers than Marlboro, both in terms of demographics as well as psychographics. Basic smokers were not coming from premium brands but from the discount category, people who wanted a good quality cigarette for a reasonable price.

It was very clear to me that Basic was not hurting Marlboro, and I considered it my responsibility to prove it to Geoff Bible and the other C-suite executives. Thankfully, it was a successful meeting. They all agreed that Basic should remain one of the top four brand priorities for Philip Morris. My relief was palpable, although my confidence in our brand strategy had never been in doubt.

We had positioned Basic very carefully. When we launched the brand, we decided that we would not pay any trade allowance to the distributors, nor would we support the brand through price promotion or coupons. Instead we decided that we would build the Basic brand at a 20 percent higher price than the rest of the discount brands and at a 20 percent lower price than the premium brands. I figured that 10 percent of the price differential should be invested in marketing dollars for building the brand. Based on this model, I asked the C-suite to allocate marketing resources for Basic. In addition, I made a commitment to Bill Campbell, the president of the tobacco business, that I'd build the Basic brand by differentiating it from every other brand in the marketplace. To this day, Basic remains the second largest brand at Philip Morris.

We positioned Basic on an anti-establishment platform. The advertising poked fun at people who pay a high price for quality products. One of the early advertising campaigns (conceived by the Leo Burnett agency), for example, included an ad that said "Your Basic Three Piece Suit" and it showed jeans, T-shirt, and sneakers. The tag line was "Tastes great costs less." Another ad said "Your Basic smoking jacket" and it showed a jean jacket. We played on the word Basic and made it a simple proposition for a quality product at a reasonable price. The brand positioning was brilliant and it worked. The smokers who bought Basic were down-to-earth, blue-collar workers.

The important thing was that we knew our consumers inside out. We spoke to tens of thousands of consumers every year in a variety of ways. We did periodic research with thousands of consumers and prospects. We had more than 2,500 people on a panel that we spoke to every month, and we also had a quarterly tracking study. In addition, we spoke to thousands of consumers all around the country, one-on-one or in small groups. We had a quarterly temperature check with the consumers to see that what we were delivering through the value proposition was relevant to them. This research was done where the brand was strong as well as among consumers who did not buy the brand. We wanted to understand why they didn't buy. We built robust research methodologies to assess consumer wants and aspirations. This not only helped us in growing the market share but also helped us ensure we didn't cannibalize the Marlboro brand. The more you know your customers, the better equipped you are to survive the fishbowl.

In Search of DNA

I employed many of the same skills when I arrived at Pitney Bowes 10 years later (has it really been that long?). The basics of marketing are timeless. First, we talked to about 2,000 customers, primarily one-to-one. We also talked to them in focus groups, and we did a lot of quantitative studies. We had 2,000 customers telling us, "You're just putting a stamp on the envelope." Except they did not know the wide capabilities that we have inside Pitney Bowes. They said that our company was not business critical to their needs. We were just there. Just there? Pitney Bowes, we heard, was like a light fixture—it's just there. We found there was very little understanding of integrated mail and document management, especially among the C-suite. Why was all this important? We started out as a postage meter company, just putting stamps on an envelope, but we thought we'd come a long way from that. So it was a blow to discover, years later, that our customers thought that was all we ever were: the postage meter company.

But that was not the reality of the situation. We were all about postage meters, sure; but we were so much more. We've evolved from our humble beginnings, just as I imagine your own business has grown from its own modest start. Your business is probably very diversified. So is our business. Some 40 percent to 50 percent of our business comes from a lot of other things—software, services, solutions. What happened to the stamp on the envelope? It's still a nice cash generator for us, but there are a lot of other things that we have going for our corporation.

There were wide variances globally of how customers understood our capabilities—Italy, Germany, and Canada saw "different" companies when they told us about Pitney Bowes. Customers in some countries saw us as a low-tech company—despite the high-tech reality about our systems and products. But it wasn't all bad news. Among the negatives we found some positives—some nuggets of purest gold. What some of our best customers told us was that we understood documents and communication flows. And in a world that's absolutely brimming with both, that's no small thing.

All this opened our eyes. We began to understand our own company through the perceptions of customers. The revelation, learned in large measure from what our many customers said, was that Pitney Bowes creates, produces, distributes, stores/retrieves, receives/integrates/manages documents. In time, we extrapolated from this to create a new tag line now often attached to our logo "Engineering the flow of communication."™ That's what we do for a living; we're not just a postage meter company. And, once that key learning was in place, it's amazing how our momentum to move the market and the other great sweet spot goals evolved.

The Human Side of Research

If you're close to consumers you stand a chance of giving them what they want. Google's forte has been, from the start, its ability to make research "more human" than any other search engine.

Google's ability to structure and process searches is so melded into the way most people would like it to be that it is no surprise that Google continues to win surveys of customer satisfaction, year after year. Not much has changed since *CRMToday* said, "Google is the run-away leader in terms of customer loyalty and satisfaction with a vast majority of study participants indicating that Google is their primary search engine and 89 percent indicating they had a strongly positive experience with the site."[3] A survey by the Keynote firm found that "Google is still king of the Web when it comes to search, and wins consumers' praise in relatively new search categories, such as image search, and continues to perform well in the more established search categories."[4]

A while ago some of Google's product development people came to talk to me about ad testing. This proved to me that they are constantly seeking to innovate and it also provided an insight into the new marketing reality. The ad testing they talked about was amazing. In the past, you'd run an ad and it would take a few months—anywhere from three to six months—to collect proper and useful feedback on the ad. Google can test ads in three weeks. This is great for marketers but is guaranteed to strike fear into every creative person in the land: They have to deliver.

Segment Your Market *Sweetly*

As you get to know more and more about your consumers there is a process at work. As you mine the minds of consumers you dig deeper and deeper. Along the way you uncover pure marketing gold: sweet segments. If—and it is a big if—you can really understand individual consumer segments, then your products and services can be tailored to fit the needs and requirements of the segments. You can achieve perfect alignment.

Segmentation is hard work. Never be fooled by the neatness of the segments that eventually emerge. All the math whizzes who are employed in marketing are looking at two things: How do we segment the consumers? And, what kind of offer and through which medium can I persuade them to buy my product?

Wal-Mart, whose fulsome embrace of the marketing discipline is still in its early stages, segments its customers into those who shop frequently with the chain in multiple categories; those who shop frequently in selective categories; and those who shop infrequently in selective categories. Its goal is to increase the selective category to multiple categories and increase their usage from infrequently to frequently.

One of my first and best segmentation experiences occurred when I was working in the ad industry in the 1980s. After six months at the ad agency Young & Rubicam (Y&R), I was officially designated as "smart" and promoted to work on the Ford Motor Company account. Believe me, this was a big deal—for me anyway. I worked alongside seasoned marketers from Y&R's New York headquarters. Joe Plummer, known for his lifestyle research methodologies for marketing; Satish Korde, a very impressive young, thoughtful, and brilliant strategist; and John Sanders, the deputy head of Y&R Detroit, were all part of the team. This was Satish's entree into the Ford business. Years later, he became the head of Ford's business at Y&R and now, as the vice chairman of WPP (which owns Y&R), heads all Ford-related business. Effectively, he is in charge of all the advertising for the Ford Motor Company.

Ford's problem was that it was under attack from Asian car manufacturers who made better-quality and more fuel-efficient cars. Quite a problem. (And one that hasn't gone away.) To make matters worse, Ford's worldwide strategy and ambition was not aligned with its product and marketing capabilities. In Europe, Ford was regarded as a low-price brand. Thanks to the Lincoln franchise, in the United States, Ford was perceived to be a luxury carmaker. The two were misaligned. And then came Ford's new strategy. This was to move upstream to the luxury market in Europe and battle the Japanese manufacturers in the United States in the mid-size segments.

None of this made a lot of sense—from where I was standing at least. So we looked at different customer segments and their behavior. We conducted ethnographic studies to understand the customers' lifestyle better. We looked at every customer's buying pattern, living style, entertainment approach, and the reasons why customers buy cars both in Europe and America. We even looked in their refrigerators to see the kind of food they ate.

Along the way we found a few surprises. (One German buyer had a fridge filled with chocolate. He explained that chocolate had uses other than eating—but that's another story.)

After studying the consumers in-depth, we segmented them into four groups: Innovators, Succeeders, Mainstream, and Laggards.

1. *Innovators* are always the first on the block to buy a new product. They like products for their innovative features and technological advances. They can be gadget freaks. They like to customize the products to fit their need. They are also willing to pay top dollar for their products. They buy Porsches.

2. *Succeeders* are driven by the need to purchase the best and the top of the line. They are also willing to pay top dollar for their products and are luxury driven. They buy products that shout success. They bought cars like Lincoln and Cadillac before the Japanese carmakers introduced Lexus and Infinity.

3. *Mainstreams* buy a good quality product with the best value. They do not buy products for prestige but for use. They buy the most fuel-efficient products. They buy the most comfortable products that have been tried in the marketplace. Quality is very important to them. They are the ones who buy Toyota, Honda, and Nissan in droves. This was also the staple for Ford and GM carmakers. This segment was very important for Ford and it was losing drastically in this group.

4. *Laggards* are the utilitarians. They look at something purely from the utility standpoint. They want cars primarily for transportation. They spend the least amount necessary and sometimes buy used cars.

Applying the Segments

We applied this segmentation to Ford cars worldwide. It became very clear that Ford didn't have the range of products to reach all the different types of audience. It wanted to sell upscale cars in Europe, but it didn't have any offerings that would appeal to that market segment. The Lincolns were too big for the European roads, so Ford could not export Lincoln. Yet, Ford wanted to reach Succeeders in Europe through its product offerings.

This meant that Ford needed to build an upscale brand in Europe. This was virtually impossible given the brand image Ford had in Europe. It is very hard to take products from mass to class. It is always easier to take products from class to mass. Ford in Europe was primarily known for mass brands, and they appealed to the Mainstreamers.

This was one of the reasons that Ford acquired "class" brands in Europe from Aston Martin to Jaguar and now Volvo. The company decided to penetrate the marketplace through acquisition, not by selling its existing Lincoln lines in Europe or starting a new platform in the United States and exporting it to Europe and the rest of the world.

At the same time, our analysis suggested Ford was known for the mid-size cars that appeal to the Mainstreamers in Europe. We thought that the U.S. market could benefit if we brought in the European mid-sized cars. That was the genesis of Ford's global product development vision.

On paper, it looked like a good strategy. But making this into a reality was very hard. Most of the car designers took tremendous pride in their designs and they were highly motivated to bring the cars to the American roads. Now we were asking them to forget their own ideas, get the mid-sized cars from Europe, agree to assemble them in the United States, and sell them through the dealerships here.

The New Segmentation

Historically, market segments were based on demographics. The age, sex, education, income, and so on, of consumers was the guid-

94

ing light. This data is still vital, but it is no longer enough. As Daniel Yankelovich and David Meer note in their *Harvard Business Review* article "Rediscovering Market Segmentation":

> *Segmentation can do vastly more than serve as a source of human types, which individually go by such colorful monikers as High-Tech Harry and Joe Six-Pack and are known collectively as by the term "psychographics." Psychographics may capture some truth about real people's lifestyles, attitudes, self-image, and aspirations, but it is very weak at predicting what any of these people is likely to purchase in any given product category. It thus happens to be very poor at giving corporate decision makers any idea of how to keep the customers they have or gain new ones.*
>
> *The failings of psychographics, however, and the disappointments it has produced in its users should not cast doubt on the validity of careful segmentation overall. Indeed, marketers continue to rely on it, and line executives increasingly demand segmentations that the whole enterprise can put into action. . . . Good segmentations identify the groups most worth pursuing—the underserved, the dissatisfied and those likely to make a first time purchase, for example.[5]*

Segmentation works and has to work now more than ever. When you get close to consumers you now have to look at:

How they behave: Look at the data surrounding each and every consumer transaction with you. How often do consumers buy your product? What else do they buy? What additional services are they looking for? What kind of pricing promotion would help them to purchase the products/services? Are they buying a single product or a bundle?

How they think: Consumers have attitudes. Get deeper under the surface and you can look at the ability of consumers to pay, their level of engagement with your products, their attitude to risk, what they believe about your products, and much more. Depending on the industry, this type of segmentation also typically looks at the values, attitudes, and lifestyle of consumers.

What they need: Can the needs of consumers be connected to the value of the products and services you sell? If you have mined consumer minds, you can calculate the lifetime value of a customer and come up with an ROI that steers you in the direction of the consumers it is best to pursue. Think 80/20: most companies struggle to find the 20 percent of consumers that provide the lion's share of the value. Segmentation can lead you there.

Using on these basic approaches, you can define hundreds of customer segments. And then, thanks to technology, you can personalize your message to them and then get desired results.

Segmentation leads to high personalization. Look at how GM uses technology that allows marketers to personalize and color print on demand. The company starts with the database generated by the GM card and adds information from its GM owner database to model its customers individually. As a result, it creates personalized messages for potential customers at the times they are most likely to be looking for new vehicles. And once a customer expresses interest, GM creates a fulfillment kit with brochures and materials individualized for that potential buyer. For instance, if a person is looking for a Corvette, he may receive a glossy solicitation of a sprightly, yellow Corvette when he is making the buying decision. Altogether—through personalization and color print-on-demand technology—GM has been able to double its mail response rate. At the same time, it has significantly decreased the cost of those offers.

And GM isn't alone. Lexus, BMW, Disney, and a host of other companies do much the same—sometimes better.

Offer Solutions with Savvy—And a Smile

Ralph Waldo Emerson, the American philosopher, once commented that the only way to have a friend is to be one. Now that may seem an odd insight to convey to someone who's interested in marketing, but it does capture a salient point. Who are your best friends? I'm willing to bet that anyone who meets your own best-friend criteria does at least two things for you that the 5,000 plain old acquaintances in your life do not. Best friends are almost always people who are willing to listen to you, your needs, your desires, your dreams, your concerns and insecurities. Then, a true best friend offers his or her experience, knowledge, and talents to help you. And all of this is done—not with the imperious scolding of a know-it-all big brother—but with the arm-on-the-shoulder smile that a loving, caring friend offers.

So, you see: All that preparation you made to learn everything you could about your own company (what each product line is capable of doing, tech specs, delivery schedules, production flows, etc.) is not wasted just because you don't open every customer conversation with a recitation of all that you know. On the contrary, when you have a firm grasp on the priority needs of your customer, that's when you can proffer your savvy to a customer who, at that time, will be all ears.

More than that, it's important to connect how the products and services your company offers can not only help your customer; you need to assure him that, above all other ways to address his problems, your solutions will satisfy him. You are selling solutions not products or services.

Michael Bosworth with John Holland wrote *Customer Centric Selling.* I really like the point they make in the opening chapter of that work. They talk about the desperate need so many marketers have to do their job "better":

> *Better in that you will stop thinking in terms of your products and their features, and start thinking in terms of your buyers and their goals, problems, and needs. Better in that you will stop forcing products on buyers, and instead start allowing them to convince themselves of their need for your offerings. Better in that you will stop giving long-winded, opinion-laden speeches to lower-level "buyers," and instead begin to have no-nonsense, results-oriented business conversations with decision makers.*[6]

97

This is especially true of business-to-business companies where there is tremendous competition from product suppliers. This makes differentiation of the product hard—as there is a tendency to compete on price alone, creating a commodity market. So how do you create differentiation to charge a premium for your product? The answer is solution selling. Solutions involve creating a judicious combination of various products and services. It is an approach that requires a large commitment in service. And this creates a customized response to customers' problem that is unique and cannot be easily copied by competition. As a result, it becomes hard and costly for customer companies to switch to competitors because in most cases it requires integrating a large number of products and services.

Once you have opted for solution selling, how do you transform your organization to deliver it? Solution selling is inherently different from product selling. The key is to promote the benefits and full value of the total solution. This is tough. And it is even harder to transform the sales force to solution selling.

At Pitney Bowes, when we started the transformation, we focused on the Enterprise Relationship Group, the group responsible for our largest customers. We brought the group together to go through a laddering process through which we taught them to start with the product and services attributes—then think about the benefits.

Laddering (a technique I learned at Y&R) is simply a way to sell a product. You sell a product at three different levels:

1. Product attributes
2. Product benefits
   —Subjective benefit
   —Objective benefit
3. Values

The basic premise is that product attributes are rarely a differentiator. Consumers do not buy a product for its attributes.

They buy it for the benefits it provides. And in most cases, the product attributes and benefits can change with time depending on the circumstances. But the values of the people do not change and if you position a product at its values level, it will not only be relevant for consumers but also can be a major differentiator with other products in similar categories. Numerous companies have exploited this type of positioning. For example: Nike—Just Do It; Marlboro—Welcome to Marlboro Country; and GE—We Bring Good Things to Life. These are good examples of positioning based on values.

So, having been through the laddering process with the Enterprise Relation Group at Pitney Bowes, we then taught them to bundle different products and services to generate benefit. In some cases we also looked at the end-to-end solutions that generate tangible customer benefits like cutting cost, increasing revenue, improving customer loyalty, or growing profit. Once we had completed that, we laddered up to explore the values of the bundled products and services. And this is just the start of the solution selling. So you are not just selling products and services but you are fulfilling organizational and human needs. Big difference: big differentiator.

So you start solution selling by identifying the customer needs. Then you involve different parts of your organization to craft a customized solution by integrating distinctive offerings for that customer. Most companies are not quipped to integrate different offerings to find a solution for an organizational need. In response, a large industry has been created—spanning consultants to integrators—to complete business process outsourcers.

So I would argue that solutions are best delivered if, per your own well-honed savvy, you feel that you can help a prospective customer with his needs. And while I think that you should always address customers with the attitude of someone who's smiling helpfully, the real test of how well you are doing your job is whether your customers' smiles catapult your own company into sweet spot status.

Hardwire Your Team to Your Customer

A friend of mine shared the story of a charismatic insurance executive who read an entire book about treating customers right and put a handful of words from the book to work as his personal leadership agenda for an entire year. The name of the executive is not of consequence; he has retired and his former company has been acquired. But when this executive read Richard Whiteley's *The Customer-Driven Company*, the vice president was magnetically drawn to nine words (out of a book of many thousand words). What did Whiteley write that had such a powerful effect? He urged his readers to "saturate your company with the voice of the customer."[7]

Based on those nine words, the executive started a campaign inside his own company. He challenged everyone in an all-employee meeting to ponder the significance of that phrase. He then went to small group sessions to beg employees to think about the tone, pitch, emotion, and logic of their own customers as they did their work that day. Even in his own staff meeting, surrounded by other senior executives, he demanded to know the last time each of them had actually spoken with a customer and whether that dialogue had registered to such a degree that it affected, positively, their decision making as supervisors. This went on for about a year. In sum, that veteran insurance executive used nine words to form a leadership agenda that lasted for months. When he went to meetings, inside or outside his own organization, he found that he no longer needed speech notes in three-ring binders. In fact, he didn't need any presentation materials at all. He just opened every speech with those nine words, amplifying in his own expressions, why the sentiment of saturating your company with the voice of the customer was indispensable to business success as he saw it. And it soon became indispensable wisdom to everyone reporting to this vice president.

So what, exactly, did that insurance executive do?

He took the generic concept of "focus on your customer" and brought it to life by making sure that everyone inside his company started acting as if their customers were ordering their priorities and actions. It was a huge value shift for that insurance company. Instead of thinking about how they would like to run their company, so they would be pleased—now they had to think about how they would run the company so their customers would be pleased. In today's techno parlance, I am seconding the thought by arguing that you have to hardwire your entire team of managers and employees so that they, too, are running your company as your customers would want it to be run. Set this one task as Job One, and you will be amazed at all the operational processes that will dramatically shift, perhaps not overnight, but in time as people think first and foremost about all that they have learned about your customers.

Communicate Consistently, with One Voice

Here, too, a story from Pitney Bowes will speak to many of you who work in companies with a diversified, international matrix of business units and divisions. At one time, Pitney Bowes had something like 10 or 11 business units. And each of the business units had their own way of marketing, their own way of broadcasting information about their products and services, their own way of looking at and talking to the marketplace. Guess what? These different approaches were, well, different.

One day I decided to reserve a huge conference room in which I put up every communication that goes out from Pitney Bowes, from all its different parts. I even forced the top 35 executives to walk through that maze of verbal data. In the end, I called it our "wall of shame." We really worked through the implications of such a chaotic approach to marketing our message; at times in the discussion, I wasn't sure if I had started to work for one company or for multiple companies. In the end, I'm happy to say that we agreed to unify our approach even if we don't always insist on every division having the same message.

Don't underestimate the importance of having one marketing approach. Again, if you will just think as your customers think, you'll see why it's important to unify the voice that you use to tell the world about who you are, what you do, what you believe, and how you would like to serve people. The message is simple: Create a succinct value proposition that focuses on customer values and product benefits rather than product attributes and then make sure everyone knows it and communicates it at every opportunity.

Share What Your Customer Would Consider "News"

At Pitney Bowes, we not only talked to customers large and small, we also interviewed about 100 journalists. Sad to say, very few of the reporters we talked to really understood our business. My goodness, one said, "Pitney Bowes, you must be an aircraft engine maker." They were confusing us with, perhaps, the turbine engine manufacturer, Pratt & Whitney.

The real damage done was not in journalists being confused. It was in journalists being bored. Think about the problem: 100 journalists, in many ways, the opinion leaders of the world—and none excited about our company. They could, if they were inspired, tell the whole world what Pitney Bowes is all about. But even the most informed journalists offered up this lackluster appraisal: "There really is no drama in your company or your industry; so why would I write about you?" You know, if you can answer that question, you can also find another entrée into the minds of your customers.

What had Pitney Bowes done poorly up to that point? Well, it wasn't forgetting to innovate. And it wasn't that we didn't know how to diversify. Recall once more that postage meters comprised only about half of our business. What we did poorly was tell the world why it should be as excited as we were each time we made a technological breakthrough, or added a business line, or invented an imaginative solution to a critical customer dilemma. We weren't getting the news out. Sound familiar?

To change this means that, starting with your existing customers, you must get the word out about what you're doing that's "news." At Pitney Bowes we really worked hard at getting our story out there. If you have a great story to tell, tell it. We have really reaped rewards with lots of opinion-changing column inches.

Remember, novelty, like beauty, is in the eye of the beholder. Telling Coca-Cola that your company has just invented a new way to process the financing of automobiles will do nothing but generate a look on your customer's face that roughly mirrors the look of anyone who's just downloaded 500 spam e-mails. If you know your customer's industry as well as his priorities, it should not be hard to filter the journalistic wheat and chaff about your company. (And, by the way, don't forget to clue in the real journalists as well!)

The next challenge, of course, is how to keep your customers up-to-date about you. Here, too, an imaginative marketer is quite probably the sweet spot marketer as well. The opportunities are legion. Consider direct marketing, telemarketing, interactive marketing, community marketing (such as My Space), search engine optimization, blogs, podcasts, viral marketing, partnerships with others in the channels, and a host of other possibilities.

What's important is to make sure that you share your company's news in ways that are both relevant and personal to your customer base. In sum, you need to communicate with people only in ways that are appropriate to them, and about products and services that they are interested in. I talked to the vice president of marketing in one major telecom company, who said his sole job was getting the right content to consumers through the right channel.

Build a Relationship

Anyone who's doing business with you now could be doing business with someone else tomorrow. That's not always the case, but I'd say, increasingly, no one has the benefit of a monopoly market. Pick your product or service, and choices abound. Even Microsoft, which once was akin to a kind of software monarchy, has to worry now about competitors like Linux and Google.

But this is more about you than about Microsoft—though a $43 billion company needs to worry just as much. You really should examine how often, and to whom, and in what ways, you say thank you to your customers. This is a good time to remind you that you should take all of my advice in this section with an appreciation for the 80/20 principle. Remember that, in almost all cases I've observed, companies generate 80 percent of their revenue (if not profits) from 20 percent of their customers. Give "thank you priority" to that precious 20 percent. This should be an organized effort, with some kind of thank you log updated regularly. It's so easy for the sentiment of thanks to lapse into a monthly series of "I meant to call" or "I meant to write" excuses. Don't let it happen to you. Your customers deserve better.

Chris Denove and James Power have done exhaustive research on customer satisfaction; and when I read about their studies (their book is called, simply, *Satisfaction*), I was struck by a statistic they cited. Denove and Powers took some of their own customer satisfaction surveys and compared the results over a five-year timeline. What they were wondering was—of the many variables that affect corporate success—whether customer satisfaction had any kind of direct bearing on the growth of companies. Now, before I share the rest of the story, allow me to ask you to bring to mind three big customers that you believe your company has not served as well as it could. Indeed, let me ask you to think about three big customers your company has quite probably disappointed sometime over the last five years. Okay, now hear this.

Denove and Powers, checking their own databank of customer satisfaction surveys, came to this conclusion:

> *What we discovered surpassed our most optimistic expectations. The relationship between satisfaction and shareholder value wasn't just visible: it was paramount! We divided each company into one of three groups: (1) companies whose customer satisfaction rank within their industry remained constant; (2) those whose rank improved; and (3) those whose satisfaction ranking dropped relative to their industry competitors. . . . The companies that improved customer satisfaction increased their shareholder value by more than 50 percent! And those whose rank declined actually lost 22 percent of their value over the previous five years.*[8]

Many a marketing professional has fallen on this sword. They acquired a new, significant business relationship by doing all the right things. They familiarized themselves with the industry, worked feverishly to learn their customer's priorities, communicated in the right way and in many ways for a long duration—and booked a bundle of business. Then, in essence, they said, "Goodbye." All right, they didn't say those words exactly, but what they did was tantamount to saying that. Because what these marketers did was abandon their attentiveness to their newly won customers and start foraging the world for more customers. And more. And more.

Overcoming the Noise

I know that understanding your customer is time-consuming and sometimes plain dull. But nuance here will not convey how strongly I feel about this sweet spot tool, which must be well used (and deployed often) for your company to acquire increased success. So let me be blunt: If you don't cut through the noise generated 24/7 by a topsy-turvy marketplace teeming with lots of hungry competitors by delivering exactly, precisely, emphatically, and economically what customers want when they want it, they will walk away. The only way to find out what your customers want, then, is to mine their minds with as much concern as you mind your own business.

Sweet Spotter: JetBlue

I may live to regret this, but I think you have to stick your neck out if you write a book like this one. (After all, that's what necks are for!) I'd like to spotlight one company in this and the next four chapters that I feel has a real shot at sweet spot status. So here goes. I would put my sweet spot light on the no-frills (beaucoup thrills!) airline JetBlue. Here's why.

It's All about Service

Airlines are notoriously tough businesses to manage, and earning a profit running an airline is even harder. But if you haven't ridden a JetBlue flight, suffice it to say that it's led by a founder-CEO of rare mettle, David Neeleman.[9] Though the airline is six years old, with 400+ flights daily to 36 cities in the western hemisphere, Neeleman talks about the need to be better, to grow his airline beyond the billion-dollar business it already is. But the one place he's not willing to change is in the area of customer service: "Although we have many changes on the horizon," Neeleman says, "one thing that won't change . . . is the great customer service you can expect at JetBlue. Every single JetBlue crew member is dedicated to making sure your flight on JetBlue is the very best you'll ever take." Fly with them and you get a better idea of the attitude they bring to customer service. And it is service with attitude and personality; it is the real thing rather than the ersatz service you receive in so many other places.

Seems that Neeleman and team mined their customers' minds very, very well. Caroline Mayer, of the *Washington Post*, notes that her experience with JetBlue has been uniformly satisfying: "Not only were the attendants friendly and helpful, but the food was more plentiful—and better—than the paltry selection [a competing airline] offered on a flight four times as long. First, everyone got a CAN of soda. And then a choice of snacks—and the attendants encouraged us to take more than one, even a selection so we could have salty nuts and sweet cookies. Admittedly, these are small issues in the world of customer service, but the small issues add up."[10]

Indeed they do. (And while I'm waxing lyrical about airlines, I should mention an Indian airline that I recently flew with—Jet Airways. The food is fantastic.) JetBlue is obviously doing a lot of things right. It won multiple *Conde Nast Traveler's* 2005 Business Travel Awards,[11] and it captured the highest "in overall airline customer satisfaction among major U.S. air carriers, according to the J.D. Power and Associates 2005 Airline Satisfaction Index Study."[12]

They Really Get the Job Done

The business school, Wharton, honored the airline with a profile in its online strategic management journal. Titled "The Steady, Strategic Ascent of JetBlue Airways," the journal gives the perspective of David Barger, who is JetBlue's president and chief operating officer. To be sure, Barger, like Neeleman, knows that JetBlue is nothing if it loses touch with its customers' needs. Per Wharton:

> *JetBlue has tried to combine the best features of low-fare carriers like Southwest, and traditional ones like United and American. Like Southwest, it eschews hub airports in favor of point-to-point flights and looks for innovative ways to cut costs. Its 1,100 call-center operators, for example, don't work in a center at all, but at their homes in and around Salt Lake City. "I have had some investors ask, 'Do they have uniforms?'" Barger quips. "And I'm like, 'I have no idea whether they are wearing anything at all.'" Nor, he said, does he care—as long as they provide excellent customer service.[13]*

There Are No Second-Class Citizens

Business watcher and television personality Willow Bay wrote her own encomium about JetBlue in *Reader's*

Digest. Again, at the heart of the article is Neeleman advocating the wisdom of heeding, not herding, your customers. He's quoted as saying, "Airlines have for so long treated people like they were an inconvenience. . . . We want to eliminate all those aggravating things that drive [passengers] crazy." So, how does he know what those things are? Bay reports, as do other sources, that Neeleman not only works alongside some of his 10,000 JetBlue employees regularly, but he also flies on his own jets as a passenger. And guess what he talks to all those customers about? (Nothing original in this—Richard Branson does it, as does Stelios Haji-Ionnanou, chief of EasyJet, but an awful lot of airline CEOs don't.)

Due to the financial dive of so many airlines since 9/11, JetBlue is a relatively good performer. If you had invested $1,000 at the start of 2003, you'd be down a couple hundred dollars going into 2006. Soaring fuel prices have hurt JetBlue; they've hurt other airlines more. But Neeleman isn't pessimistic, and neither am I. Who can turn their back on an airline whose motto is "No first-class seats, no second-class citizens"? JetBlue has 189 more planes on order, and I plan to board them whenever I can. Or as Neeleman says himself: "Thank you for flying JetBlue and I look forward to meeting you onboard one of our flights soon."

Demarcating Demand

Sweet Spot Skill #2: Avoid "everybody" traps; they'll lead you where everyone else is heading. Reinvent your marketplace. Link your seller specs to the buyer's specs—then add a tad more. Build competitive moats.

"If a man can write a better book, preach a better sermon, or make a better mousetrap than his neighbor," said American essayist Ralph Waldo Emerson more than 100 years ago, "though he build his house in the woods, the world will make a beaten path to his door."[1] This indeed is the spirit of many great engineers I know. And a sizeable number of manufacturing chiefs go to bed each night praying this is true. I've even known more than a few chief executives who bet the proverbial ranch on the sentiment. But a marketer—especially a sweet spot marketing leader—knows better. It's about more than the mousetrap. It's about demarcating, actually creating the map, for the demand needed not only to sustain a good mousetrap manufacturer but, indeed, to make that enterprise the envy of all other competitors.

Think Google

Now, how many times have you read a news story about disgruntled stockholders badgering the likes of some CEO, even one as esteemed as Jack Welch during his days at GE? No chief executive is, or should be, immune from challenges. But I love seeing that rare headline that heaps praise on executive leadership. For example, here's how one story was headlined: "Google Shareholders Praise Management."[2] Although the annual meeting of Google stockholders, on May 11, 2006, did have its moments of brief friction, most of the meeting was ebullient. In the report, Oakland, California, resident Jack Easterling was very much the theme-setter: "I am happy with the way the company is performing." But it's not that shareholders like Easterling are happy; it's why he and so many others are happy.

Here's a company that created $55 billion in investor wealth in just one year, but it was not by selling one mousetrap. If Google had taken its slim, trim search engine format and sat still, I can guarantee you that Easterling and others would be lambasting Google's leadership. But try this exercise for me, will you? Open up Google and type in "What is Google?" You'll quickly find a list that goes on for several web pages. Google is search. Google is talk. Google is maps and satellite imaging. Google is e-mail. Google is group interaction. Google is scholastic research. Google is news . . . enough, you get the point.

Google knew, when its search engine became such a popular commodity, that standing still would be lethal. So the main reason that so many stockholders are happy is that they know that the search engine results for "What is Google" will be different, and quite probably, better (and stronger!) at the next annual meeting. From the report, this quote tells the story better than I possibly can: "Google CEO Eric Schmidt assured shareholders that Google is working diligently to develop even more products to build upon the company's success story, which included a $592 million profit on revenue of $2.25 billion during the first three months of this year. 'We have lots more stuff coming,' Schmidt said. 'The rate of innovation and impact of Google is just beginning.'"

Demarcate Forces

Sweet spot companies invent the marketplace in which they can win first, best, and most often. Think of Coca-Cola reinventing its marketplace as "refreshment" rather than fizzy drinks; or Visa regarding its competition as cash as well as other credit cards.

Apple was long known as a niche computer company, specializing in computers for the educational market, designers, graphic artists, and some publishing houses. This capped its market at 10 percent or less of all computer users. Apple knew it needed to grow in order to survive—but how?

As it turned out, Apple's first shot at expansion was a new operating system, blessed as OS X in 2000, that incorporated all the user-friendly look-and-feel of its original system but using a UNIX-based technology that made it more acceptable to the huge business market. Soon thereafter, Apple introduced the iPod revolution. In short, Apple's strategy was to appeal to a wider base of computer users and simultaneously create a whole new base of digital music fans. But to do this, it had to redraw its marketplace map. The myriad computers and laptops and printers all had to be pared to focus on Apple's future. Apple's CEO (and co-founder) Steve Jobs put it this way: "It comes from saying no to 1,000 things to make sure we don't get on the wrong track or try to do too much. We're always thinking about new markets we could enter, but it's only by saying no that you can concentrate on the things that are really important."[3]

I recall the first time we found out, from our surveys, that only 6 percent of our customers bought more than one product, service, or software from Pitney Bowes. Reverse that discovery: 94 percent of our customers only had one product or service. Which means that a large part of Pitney Bowes was (1) spending most of their time focused on a very wide arc of small-scale business, and (2) that we were not yet skilled at deciding what were our strongest marketplace offerings and then communicating that much more broadly throughout our customer base. With increasing emphasis on cross-selling, we've addressed that situation quite substantially now, and our performance is the better for it.

Here's another example from my own experience: this time in toothpaste. I first met Rueben Mark, chairman of Colgate Palmolive, in the late 1980s. I was working for the advertising agency Young & Rubicam (Y&R) at the time, and had just been transferred from working on Y&R's largest business, Ford Motor Company, to its second largest business to run the advertising of Colgate oral care. At his company's annual shareholder meeting, Mark praised Y&R's work on Colgate's tartar control toothpaste—he knew a sweet spot when he saw it. He also knew the tartar control category offered a way to close the gap with Procter & Gamble's market-leading toothpaste Crest.

I started on the Colgate business when the agency was heavily involved in launching the tartar control category. We had been working on the launch for a while. The product had to get Food & Drug Administration (FDA) approval. And the FDA had not approved the claim of efficacy for tartar control. So we could talk about efficacy through reference only and not directly. In other words, we could not say that tartar control toothpaste can help in reducing the germs in your mouth. This was a big challenge for us. How do you introduce a new category that can not make the efficacy claim of reducing diseases? The claim had to be cosmetic and not related to the health benefit directly. So, we decided that the new campaign for Colgate tartar control toothpaste would be based on something that really mattered to consumers—not just the benefits level as it had been in the past. Based on this insight, one of the young creative directors proposed a "vignette" campaign—showing consumers in various situations using Colgate toothpaste. The pay off for the campaign was: "We love to see you smile." This was an instant hit with the agency and the C-suite of Colgate Palmolive. The campaign helped establish a new category in oral care—tartar control. Colgate had found a sweet spot by moving the market.

Before tartar control, Colgate trailed Crest in market share. But by 2000, Colgate's share had leapt to 37 percent—passing its rival. By moving the market, Colgate had found a way to close the gap on Crest.

Demarcating demand is by no means a fixed-forever arrangement. Sweet spot companies are more than willing to shift their focus and to downgrade their emphasis on one line of business in favor of one that they feel has the better chance of growing. This is true even for FedEx. The company that started with absolutely, positively overnight aspirations has evolved to a company that actually delivers more packages via multiday, on-the-ground delivery systems.

Closely attached to this point is that sweet spot companies need an enormous amount of data collection and discussion in order to decide which way to take the company. The importance of all employees knowing what the company is all about, in terms of market emphasis, has never been more important. It may seem a paradox, but the tighter the corporate focus, the looser the company can be in raising the ceiling on the areas of market focus which it commands.

Other sweet spots are unpredictable. Consider the beer Corona. In the late 1990s imported bottled beer—and Corona in particular—became ultra fashionable to drink in the United States: "Vacation in a bottle." Corona took its first trip to the United States in 1979, starting out in California and Texas. By the late 1980s, the beer with a slice of lime had caught on in a big way. By 1997, it had toppled Heineken as the #1 imported beer in the United States. As sales rose from 14 million 2.25-gallon cases in 1993 to 38 million cases in 1997, a new brewery had to be built—at Zacatecas, Mexico—to meet the surge in demand. "Corona, at the rate it's going, will equal the GNP of the United States by 2010," opined one beverage analyst.

A now legendary story of a quality product coupled with great marketing, Corona even made it into the hands of Harvard Business School students—as a case study. Ironically, however, the meteoric rise of the bottled beer from Mexico caused problems for its owners. The Mexican family-owned business Grupo Modelo produces Corona beer. However, drinks giant Anheuser-Busch (AB) owns half—though not a controlling half—of the company. As Corona is the #1 imported beer in the United States, this creates a potential source of tension between AB and Modelo, a source of tension for AB at least. In 1999 it introduced its own product, Tequiza, pitched at the Corona market. To date, it has largely failed to win over U.S. consumers. In the meantime, Corona goes from strength to strength. This just goes to show that sweet spots are hard to imitate.

Veterans Hitting Home Runs

Then there are examples of sweet spots that happen almost by chance: A company gets lucky. Their market moves and customers migrate. And sweet spots are not confined to the fortunate and the young. There are examples out there of veterans hitting home-runs. There are many examples of companies and brands seemingly long past their prime rediscovering the sweet spot.

Brushed-suede Hush Puppies had been kicking around for 30-odd years before they hit the height of fashion. Introduced in 1958, they settled down to life as a safe but comfy casual shoe for the middle-aged. But, in the mid-1990s, they were rediscovered by the fashion conscious East Village crowd in New York. Clothing designer John Bartlett used the shoes as accessories in his 1995 spring collection. On the West Coast, Los Angeles designer Joel Fitzpatrick turned over an art gallery to the sale of Hush Puppies, installing a 25-foot inflatable bassett hound on the roof. Hush Puppies were transformed into urban chic.

Jazzed up in a range of brightly colored coats, the Puppies soon found their way onto the feet of the rich and trendy. Seen in the company of Friends' stars Matthew Perry, David Schwimmer, Lisa Kudrow, Matt LeBlanc, and Jennifer Aniston; Hollywood luminaries like Jim Carrey and Sharon Stone; and pop icon David Bowie, by 1996 Hush Puppies were being honored by the Council of Fashion Designers of America as top accessory of the year. And the effect on sales? In 1995, 430,000 pairs of classic Hush Puppies scampered out of the stores. In 1996, that figure swelled to 1,600,000. Sweet.

Or think of the remarkable resurgence of the Burberry brand. Burberry was an unlikely luxury brand in the otherwise middle-market portfolio of the U.K. group, GUS, whose other main interests are the retailer Argos and Experian credit information services. In the space of three years, CEO Rose Marie Bravo rescued the brand from the dusty discount bin and turned it into a major fashion brand, an ultra-hip label much favored by the celebrity in-crowd. In 1997, GUS was being advised to get rid of the business for $300 million or less. Now Burberry is valued at up to $1.5 billion.

An Apple a Day

I could easily go on, as long as I'm talking about a business spinning strong in a sweet spot zone. Think Apple. Okay, so it came up with the simplest, easiest-to-use computer interface before anyone else did. Apple plugged and played sooner than any competitor. And who came to their party? Teachers and students, mainly. That was by design. That was by market mapping. It wasn't just a simple exercise in people searching for, and finding, the better mousetrap. Check the early history of Apple and you'll find that co-founder Steve Jobs didn't pine after the business market when he was cranking up what's now a $17 billion company with close to 15,000 employees. Introducing personal computers into education was important to Jobs. Along the way he launched educational projects including Kids Can't Wait, the Apple Education Foundation, and the Apple University Consortium.[4]

Given this commitment, it wasn't all that long before Apple products became the personal favorite of teachers and professors—and, most importantly, students. That niche market carried the company for many years, but it was not enough. Apple's market share, for decades, was restricted by Apple's own priorities. Sure, they expanded somewhat into the world of publishing and graphics (artists and musicians were a strong following as well), but the reality of such demand—demarcated by Apple itself—was that its share of computer sales was always an exercise in counting single-digits.

As I noted earlier, it was not until Apple struggled into the twenty-first century that its fortunes exploded. Then again, "fortunes" is really the wrong word. Apple simply mapped a new marketing horizon for itself. It realized that it had to take its millions of happy customers and expand what they thought Apple was capable of. Apple slapped the face of the marketplace and shouted: "Hey, we not only make easy-to-use computers, we make computer towers and laptops in attractive, acrylic shells—raspberry-colored, even! Hey, we not only make easy-to-use and attractive computers, we make it possible for you to digitize your favorite songs and play them on instruments the size of a deck of cards! Hey, we not only make small-sized digital music players, we make even smaller hand-held devices that play movies and television shows! Hey, we not only make small hand-held devices that play movies and television shows, we now make computers that can boot up with our OS X system or with any operating system made by Microsoft! Hey, we not only make. . . ." And on and on it goes.

Apple is demarcating the demand for its next-generation products right now. Apple's predictable unpredictability is so compelling, you can even find some online videos that project what a customer would like Apple to build next. For example, rumors of an Apple cell phone (that performs a profusion of other functions as well) have spawned at least one online video done by a consumer, not by anyone from Apple marketing.[5] Now, that's demarcating demand!

More Cream in Your Coffee?

Okay, how about one more. You know Starbucks. You've had their coffee, plain, with cream, or in any of their hundreds of permutations that sound like, or rhyme with, Frappuccino. You know the coffee house feel with mood lighting, live music, and even conference rooms that you can rent if you'd like to host a group of coffee lovers. Then came the sandwiches and yummy desserts. Then came the Starbucks' locations in bookstores, and airports, and grocery stores. So, as crooner Peggy Lee might have phrased it: "Is That All There Is?"[6] Are you sitting down?

This story in *Promo* magazine set awhirl even my market-mapping mind:

Starbucks Enters Movie Business with Lionsgate

Starbucks Corp. is moving beyond the coffee cups and is heading for Hollywood.

The Seattle-based coffee chain is marking its first foray into the movie industry under a new deal with Lionsgate, in which it will promote the new film Akeelah and the Bee in some 5,500 stores in the U.S. and Canada. Under the partnership, Starbucks will carry the Akeelah and the Bee soundtrack and the DVD of the film when it rolls out.

Starbucks will offer screenings of the film to store baristas before its debut. The chain will also run in-store promotions, sneak previews and a Wi-Fi network promotion. Starbucks will use its relationship with XM Satellite Radio to offer special programming on its Hear Music Channel.

For it[s] support, Starbucks will receive an undisclosed amount of box-office sales from the film. The company is also considering plans to get involved in film production.[7]

The movie, which stars Laurence Fishburne among others, received good reviews. You can't help but get swept into the mood of the story even by watching the trailer.[8] And exactly how Howard Schultz and his top team (especially Nicole Denson, the director of business development for Starbucks) became fascinated with the tale of a young girl whose goal became winning a national spelling bee is still a bit of a mystery to me.[9] But it has a lot to do with how Schultz, Denson, and other executives are redefining what it means to be a coffee house. The view of Schultz was captured by Lorenza Munoz of the *Los Angeles Times:* "Starbucks chairman Howard Schultz, who is well-connected in Hollywood with a board seat at DreamWorks Animation, said the company has no plans to finance movie production. But, he added, Starbucks will continue developing entertainment-related ventures, with films a natural extension of the company's success with music. 'We can help customers discover entertainment,' said Schultz."

So, you see: Building the mousetrap is actually something that happens at the end of the line of imaginative thinking that is required to become, and stay, a sweet spot business. Which is why marketing, in this new age of business, is more essential than ever. The need for everyone inside the business (but especially those in the marketing function) to think about how to demarcate demand for pioneering new and profitable businesses is absolutely critical. And here's what I would advise any group of corporate leaders to do; it all comes down to two imperatives:

1. Define how "everybody" views your company, then forget it.

It would be irresponsible not to keep in mind, constantly, the image that you feel the world holds of your company. Yet, dwell too long on the way "everybody" thinks about your company, and you will quickly be in danger of a most-perilous disease: complacency. This is doubly dangerous if your business is robust enough—high revenues, decent profits—that you can gloat about how great your company is.

I'd bet that Sears, in the 1970s, saw itself as a paragon of sales power; indeed, top execs at the time quite probably viewed themselves as the store for the middle-class American population. Too bad that no one at the time could put aside that self-congratulatory point of view and start thinking like Wal-Mart. In just 20 years, Wal-Mart made Sears irrelevant as a competitor. In other words, Sears had at least 20 years to forget about how the store operated and start thinking about how it could operate. Such insights apply as well to manufacturers and service providers. Imagine the sad plight of any company that rested on making facsimile machines— and only fax machines. (Pitney Bowes actually had a fax business but realized that it was a commodity business so we got out of it in 2000.) They would have been swallowed whole by the companies saying that scanners, fax machines, and copiers could be integrated into one unit.

In the academic world of marketing, there is a science called *demand forecasting*. One of the experts in this field is Dr. Mark Moon, who collaboratively wrote *Sales Forecasting Management: A Demand Management Approach* with John T. Mentzer.[10] It is more of a textbook, but one can learn much from what's in the book. Mark Moon has also written a number of smaller treatises on the subject. In one, he concludes:

> *World-class forecasting is a moving target. The two things that have been constant over the last 20 years of research into forecasting practices is that nothing is static, and no company is world-class over all dimensions. Every organization has opportunities to improve on their forecasting practices. The good news is that most companies are now recognizing that excellence in supply chain management requires excellence in understanding and managing demand. Clearly, continued work needs to be done. . . .*[11]

That work begins, in my opinion, by trying to erase the popular, even universal, view of what your company makes and whom your company serves. You can't get out-of-the-box till you can get your current view of what success is completely out of your mind.

2. Make your way of doing business a moat that others cannot easily cross.

Seems like the phrase was a hotter, more frequently used term a couple of decades back: "barriers to competitive entry." In the 1980s, a lot of business scholars were preoccupied with the branch of strategic thinking that focused on how a business could literally deprive anyone else from imitating their success. Michael Porter, of Harvard, is the guru on this subject today. In his many books and numerous articles, Porter has tried to help business people think about the "five competitive forces" that help to define the attractiveness of any industry.

For anyone into deep strategic planning, Porter's work is required reading. But I prefer, in some ways, the language of the inveterate investor, Warren Buffett. So also, it appears, does Joe Mansueto, the founder of Morningstar (the mutual fund research powerhouse). When he was interviewed about his work and management philosophy by Inc.com, Mansueto said he became convinced in the viability of Morningstar because it passed the Buffett "moat" test. Said Mansueto, "Buffett looks for companies that have a 'moat' that shields them from competition and allows them to earn high rates of return. The moat is something that creates high barriers to entry for would-be competition."[12] I'm not particularly drawn to B-movies about drama and intrigue in medieval castles, but I do think the idea of a "moat" conveys a feeling that I don't always get by reading Michael Porter.

Because when you're protected by a moat (at least, back in the Middle Ages), you really could rest at night, content that the enemy wasn't going to be scaling your walls without making a great deal of noise and commotion. But as I have thought about all this in a very in-depth way—not as a theoretician or as an investor—but as someone who really has to protect and promote a corporate business, the more I have come to think that barriers to competitive entry and moats are just a tad passé. They are, to be sure, an ideal to strive for. And, in some industries, you are perhaps (as with a new cancer drug protected by a patent) secure, at last for a while. Yet the logic of Peter Rip, who's the managing director for Leapfrog Ventures in Menlo Park, California, seems most compelling to me. On one of his blogs, Rip takes the expected point of view of a venture capitalist (VC), someone hoping to bring a small business idea into a thriving reality. But read his words, if you will, with the viewpoint of anyone in any business. The logic increasingly holds:

> *This question arises in every meeting with a prospective VC investor. It is also the most vexing issue for both the VC and the company looking for an investment. If taken literally, both sides are looking for some impenetrable advantage that assures a monopoly, however tiny, for this new company. The "barrier to entry" is the small company's insurance against annihilation.*
>
> *Ain't no such thing.*
>
> *Any cursory examination of the literature on the economics of industrial organization will confirm this fact. There are no sustainable barriers—capital, brand, cost advantage, and so on, all*

evaporate over time. The evolution of technologies and buyers' tastes assures that no competitive advantage endures forever. Even government regulations and patents are not a barrier, particularly in a world awash with multiple technologies for accomplishing the same tasks.

Great words from Peter Rip, but it's the end of his blog that deserves special emphasis (italics mine): *"In the end, the only thing that is unique to your business is you. Your only real barrier to entry is your ability to stay ahead. That's what the 'barrier to entry?' conversation is really about."*[13]

The other point to be made is that brands do actually have the power of longevity. I once had a candid discussion about all this with William Kupper Jr., president of *BusinessWeek*, who shared this powerful thought: "Everything in a company depreciates. Brand is the only thing in the corporate world that can appreciate." (More of this in Chapter 7.)

So, let's recap. When I assert that sweet spot companies should build, á la Buffett, competitive moats, I am urging you to think long and hard about you, your team, your business, your processes, your attitudes, your mission, your values—I'm asking whether the uniqueness of your business is equal to the specialness of your product or service. For my own feeling is that— whether you make pill containers, or automobiles; whether you run a hotel or dig ditches—the only thing that makes you invulnerable to competitors is that you have operated your business in such a memorable, favorable, and commendable way that your customers become the people guarding your castle. Zealous customers are the best moat any business can have. And, of course, the best way to test a moat is to invite competitors to try to cross it (to court competition, in other words), something our sweet spotters routinely do. And if someone does breach the brand walls, guess what? Sweet Spot companies know they need to get back out there and dig a deeper moat.

Dell does a great job of this. You don't see anything from Dell that is not consistent. Their advertising is exclusively focused on their products. Logo, typeface, color—it's all the same, every-where in the world. Dell's web site is very functional, too. And, once customers start interacting with them, Dell gathers enough information to start a very personal dialogue. In the end, you build the computer you want to buy—not the one they want to sell you. That's an enormous difference—a deep moat. And how has Dell built such a consistent, recognizable brand? I'd argue that it has an awful lot to do with differentiating itself from the rest of the pack.

When the computer world was selling its products through stores, or through a direct salesforce, Dell did something differ-ent. They launched a web-based, built-to-order business. They fo-cused on their customers. And they've built their brand through single-minded attention to those customers. Dell's difference has enabled them to reinvent the marketplace.

Flying over Barriers to Entry

And if we're talking about breaking down barriers to entry as if they weren't there, recall Southwest Airlines. Remember the old joke: How do you create a million-dollar airline? Start with a billion-dollar airline and wait a year. The point? That the airline industry has been so competitive, so disrupted, so beset by labor strikes, takeovers, management upheavals, that it loses money. Big time.

And it's the easiest thing to do, if you want to start a conver-sation with a total stranger, to just ask if he has recently flown on an airline. "How was it?" should start a long tirade. Fair enough. Then you meet Southwest Airlines. Perhaps the best starting point for our conversation about it is this: You would not have lost money had you invested $1,000 on the first buying day of 2003. Going into mid-2006, you would have earned something like a 23 percent gain. Really! You would have lost money in just about every other airline, but not Southwest. So, in their own way, how did they become an alluring investment?

Herb Kelleher, who for years was chairman, president, and CEO of Southwest Airlines, was certainly quotable in his day. He was reported to wear a bunny suit to attract attention to his airline. But Kelleher was a very prudent bunny, as he told one publication:

> *Southwest Airlines has a reputation as the wild and crazy guy of commercial aviation. Yet in many ways we are the most conservative company in our industry. We have always maintained a strong balance sheet, watched our costs, and paid as much attention to our financial fitness in good times as in bad. That discipline lets us move quickly when opportunities come our way. From 1990 to 1994, for instance, when the airline industry lost $12.5 billion, we were able to buy more planes and enhance our capacity to compete in today's growing market.*[14]

That was 1997, but Southwest Airlines has preserved this point of view. If you want to get a feel for that, notice how—next time you fly them—it's the flight attendants who are cleaning up the plane, not a highly paid ground crew, before the next load of passengers hop on.

Southwest Airlines started in 1971; back then, the airline business was populated by many airline companies, all operating in the manner that was set in the days of Howard Hughes. However, through the turbulent 1980s and 1990s, all airlines were shaken by enormous cost structures that were no longer sustained by high ticket prices. In fact, Southwest was leading the trend to charge less (and less!) for a plane ticket. How could they do this? According to one source, the airline behaved contrary to the traditional business model. It avoided major airports, flew only point-to-point, bought one type of aircraft to standardize operations, and trained employees in a variety of functions.[15]

Many other airlines—the big birds like Delta, USAir, and American—tried to start their own version of a discount airline; but none flew as high as Southwest. Now a $7 billion business, Southwest has held to its original vision fending off all imitators. For example, in fourth quarter 2005, Southwest had a 54 percent jump in profit, while American posted a $604 million loss.[16] Southwest Airlines moved the market by creating the first successful no-frills airline, and the airline has actually dedicated a web page ("We Weren't Just Airborne Yesterday") to show it has outdated to innovate itself each year to remain a competitive force.[17]

Smoking Moats

The thing about building moats is that there can be no half measures. They are there to keep the competition out, to give the competition no chance at all. This was brought home to me when I was involved in the dramas of Marlboro's price cut on the morning of April 2, 1993. It was a Friday, and the company's top 100 executives were at an offsite meeting in a hotel conference room in Fairfax, Virginia. The doors of the conference room were locked, and Philip Morris security was posted heavily outside the room. No one could go out or come in to the conference room. Executives were being asked not to make any phone calls from the phone booths. The conference room was abuzz.

The big and incredibly well-rehearsed announcement was that the retail price of Marlboro was to be cut 20 percent in the U.S. market. It was a major shift in business strategy designed to increase market share and grow long-term market profitability in a highly price-sensitive market environment. Philip Morris also froze the prices of other premium brands to compete more effectively with the aggressively growing discount brands.

To put things in perspective, more than 124 billion Marlboro cigarettes were sold in 1992—if the year's sales were lined up end-to-end, it would stretch to the moon and back 27 times. This single brand had more revenues than the Campbell Soup Company, the Kellogg company, Gillette, or RJR Nabisco. In 1992, *Financial World* named Marlboro as the world's most valuable brand.

The day was immediately termed as "Marlboro Friday" by Wall Street, and it was heralded as a milestone in marketing history. On Marlboro Friday, the price of Philip Morris stock dropped 23 percent, wiping out $13.4 billion in shareholder equity. This was the largest one-day decline in a single stock since October 19, 1987. The stocks of most consumer products companies declined by double digits on this day as investors sold off stocks in other consumer products manufacturers such as Procter & Gamble, Coca Cola, Quaker, and others.

Was this action warranted? Some marketing gurus maintained that the program was an overreaction. One Wall Street analyst said, "They used an ax where a scalpel would have been preferable. It destroyed an industry's profitability." But they were overlooking Marlboro's steady decline. It was losing one share point per year. A loss in one share point in the cigarette industry equated to $150 million being wiped off the net profit. Discount brands were growing rapidly with over 33 share points—against Marlboro's 20. Marlboro was weakening.

Something needed to be done. The result wasn't a knee-jerk strategy. In the comparatively isolated market of Portland, the idea of a price reduction had been tested. This suggested that the brand would grow four share points if the price was reduced by 20 percent. In fact, by the end of the 1990s, Marlboro's share had doubled to over 40 share points.

What tends to be forgotten is that Marlboro Friday was a three-pronged strategy. It was a very deep moat indeed. Most observers talked about the first prong in the strategy, the dramatic price reduction. What went unnoticed was the serious brand-building effort that accompanied the headline-making price cut. I would argue that the brand-building effort was more instrumental as it not only restored Marlboro's image and stopped market share bleeding, but it also helped the brand double its market share.

The brand-building strategy was to increase marketing expenditure and to develop customer loyalty programs. It substantially beefed up the Marlboro Adventure Team Continuity Program that had originally started in October 1990. Under this program, Marlboro purchasers were awarded five miles per pack and, depending on the number of miles, could participate in an

Adventure Team Expedition and acquire Western clothing and outdoor gear featured in the Adventure Team catalog.

This strategy sent the competition scurrying in different directions with heavy casualties. The competition had no choice but to match the price of Marlboro, and that in turn reduced their profitability drastically. So when Marlboro started investing heavily in its brand building efforts, the competition had no resources left to fight back with.

The third strategy was the streamlining of the discount category and breed more profitability into the business. This resulted in the survival of the strong discount brands.

Moats and Streams

So, how did we build moats at Pitney Bowes? The first thing we said is that we have 80 percent market share. Someone said: "Why would anybody work so hard if they have 80 percent market share?" Eighty percent market share; what would happen? It's very hard to go higher than 80 percent market share, but you will never stay static; your share is likely to go down. And if you have 80 percent market share, think about all the people who work for you. If you have 80 percent market share in some areas, how hard do you think they will work? How motivated will they be to change the company? How motivated will they be to work with you on something new? So we redefined the marketplace. At the time, Pitney Bowes was about a $4 billion business, which means the industry would be about $5 or $6 billion. We expanded our view of the marketplace and said we are now operating in a $250 billion dollar industry. Our market share is not 80 percent—*but 2 percent*. Imagine the internal conflict that we went through. We were the king of the hill; now we had to be hungry for growth. That created a lot of turmoil, but it changed the way people thought about their place in the world. Suddenly growth was an imperative.

Next, we came up with a neologism to help us focus everyone in the company on what makes us a unique force in the marketplace:

Mailstream. In 2005, I was on vacation in the Himalayas. I kept looking down at the inherent beauty of a stream near where I was hiking. I recall that this idea struck me: What if Pitney Bowes added "stream" to the word "mail" because, after all, our trademark is all about engineering the flow of communication? This wasn't startlingly original; the word had been used in Pitney Bowes before. But suddenly it made sense to me. And, as you know, if you really understand something it makes it a lot easier to persuade others to join you. When I came back to work, I said, "Let's stop all other work; let's focus on Mailstream and go and test it as a new way to relate to the marketplace." Then, and now, I realize that there is no such word as "mailstream" in the dictionary, and that's why nobody knew what it was. But we can make the word mean something for our employees and for our customers. After all, Google is now a verb.

That's how we connected Pitney Bowes to Mailstream. For us, the word now means the creation and flow of mail & documents (both traditional and digital) and packages. The Mailstream is the flow of all of these into and out of your organization, and Pitney Bowes handles it through digital technology coupled with process improvements and our years of gained expertise. By the way, it's been a big hit with customers. Most people don't know what the word means (we knew that), but they are very intrigued by what it could mean for them (we love that). (See Figure 6.1.)

But how does all of this relate to Pitney Bowes taking a concept and converting it in a way that builds a competitive moat? We knew, from the start that Mailstream was going to be a competitive strength for us only if people inside the company could become "Mailstreamers." We made sure we started with those who would actually be using the word with our customers. In one-on-one sessions with people inside and outside of marketing, we drilled home the sense that Pitney Bowes is all about Mailstream and that Mailstream is all about Pitney Bowes. One equals the other. We knew quickly that we had to do more, because we got from our own people the same thing that we got from customers: intrigue, but not full and complete understanding.

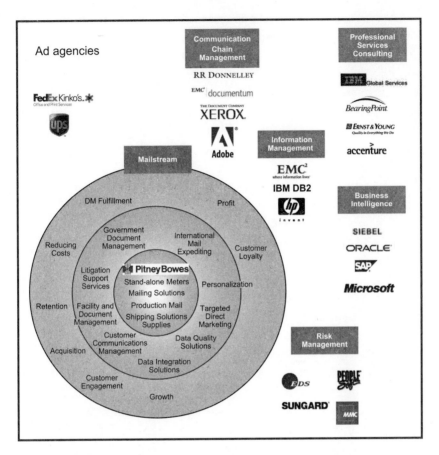

FIGURE 6.1   **Mailstream Differentiates Pitney Bowes**

In the end, through multiday offsite meetings, videos, visioning exercises, charts and graphs, and a lot of informed dialogue, I can happily report that the collective mindset inside Pitney Bowes has moved so that the company and everyone in it understands Mailstream as we define it as much as someone inside Google understands the verb "Googling." About two thirds of our sales force can now articulate what Pitney Bowes does, and at the same time more than half of our employees find Mailstream relevant. Even more remarkable is the result among customers. Mailstream awareness grew dramatically in the six

129

months of launch. There has been growth in understanding of Pitney Bowes and most of the brand attributes such as "innovative" and "technology driven" have grown substantially. In short we have established a new $250 Billion business category in a very short period of time. And that achievement is, as Peter Rip said on his blog, a real achievement, the beginning of a daunting competitive moat, because "in the end, the only thing that is unique to your business is you."

Sweet Spotter: Coldwater Creek

If you are a professional woman between the ages of 35 and 60, well educated, with money to spend, you have almost certainly heard of Coldwater Creek. If you are a marketer or an investor, and you haven't heard of Coldwater Creek, pay attention!

Coldwater Creek began in 1984 as a catalog company offering women's accessories and gifts with a Native American influence. The original catalog offered 18 items; today about 3,000 items are available. The company has expanded its operations from the kitchen table of its founders, Dennis and Ann Pence, to a 20-acre campus in Sandpoint, Idaho; a customer service center in nearby Coeur d'Alene; and a state-of-the-art distribution center in Parkersburg, West Virginia.[18]

One of the nation's fastest-growing retailers, its sales are expected to increase this year by 18 percent, to $698.4 million. Profit growth has been 137 percent over the past three years (year ending in May); profits are estimated by analysts to jump 52 percent this year.[19] From an initial offering price of $2.22 (January 30, 1997), company stock has risen to $28.50 (May 12, 2006), doubling in the past year.[20]

They Know Their Segment

So, why am I so sure that a woman meeting the criteria I mentioned earlier has heard of Coldwater Creek? Because the company understands that demographic group perfectly. They advertise in magazines aimed at that group, and they provide their customer three sales channels: catalogs, web site, and retail stores.

The small original catalog has expanded into four: Northcountry, the company's core catalog, with apparel, jewelry, accessories, and gifts; Spirit, featuring contemporary mix-and-match separates, coordinating accessories, and jewelry; Sport, offering colorful casual active wear; and Coldwater Creek, which offers a selection from the other three catalogs.[21] Last year the company sent over 100 million catalogs to its mailing list of 15 million names, of which over 2.5 million had purchased something in the last 12 months.[22]

They Communicate in Multiple Ways

Coldwater Creek also reaches customers through its web site, http://www.coldwatercreek.com, an attractive, colorful, and easy-to-navigate shopping experience. E-mails are sent frequently to registered customers, usually more than once a week. The content of these messages includes not only new merchandise available in the retail stores but also price reductions on items available online. Internet kiosks are placed in the retail stores to enable customers to order merchandise (with free shipping) available only online; this allows stores to carry only 35 percent to 40 percent of the items offered in its catalogs. The company then uses information from its online sales to determine where to open new retail stores.[23]

Aware that the increase in Internet shopping nationally is changing the retail landscape, Coldwater Creek is locating some of its new stores in so-called lifestyle centers, the open-air retail centers offering easy access to individual stores. Such centers offer convenient parking and walkways so shoppers can get in and out quickly. The company plans to expand its retail locations from 179 last holiday season to 244 by the end of fiscal 2006.[24]

They Live to Serve

Still, with much-larger competitors such as Talbot's, Ann Taylor, and Chico's seeking the same over-35 customer,[25] what makes Coldwater Creek stand out? One thing, emphatically: customer service. The company was founded with "a fierce determination to set new standards for mail order service"[26] and that focus continues today in all of its sales channels. For example, the company responds to online "Instant Help" inquiries in 10 to 15 seconds.[27]

One of my acquaintances is a fan of Coldwater Creek. She says the stores are not sterile, utilitarian places like so many other stores. "Coldwater Creek is such an attractive store. It has warm wood, ambient lighting, and a welcoming feel. The clerks are sincerely friendly and very helpful. They will help a person to pick out clothes for a special occasion, bring another size while one is in the dressing room, and suggest an alternative if something doesn't fit. The clothes are flattering to a woman over 35 and are more expressive, if you know what I mean. They're not all black, white, and taupe; on the contrary, they are quite colorful. The mood in the store is upbeat. But you know what I think I like best about the store? The staff are real women; they aren't fashion models that one could never emulate. They aren't perfect, but they are all attractive, and they are around my age. I feel comfortable in the store."

Another customer, responding to an online story about the store, said, "I love Coldwater stores and clothes. All the employees are really nice and I also notice they are very nice to each other. Store energy seems really positive. It is my favorite place to shop."[28]

Coldwater Creek has succeeded so well in its goal to please the customer that, in a poll conducted by the National Retail Federation, it was voted #1 in customer service nationally in the specialty retailer segment. It also placed in the elite list of *BusinessWeek*'s "100 Best Small Companies."[29]

It has come a long way from the days when its founder, Dennis Pence, used to ride his bicycle two miles to the UPS office to avoid the package pickup fee. "We really didn't know what we were doing," recalls Pence, "but we had great confidence in ourselves."[30] Pence may still ride his bicycle, but his company is riding much, much higher.

From Logo to Icon

Sweet Spot Skill #3: Brands are the heart and soul of sweet spot companies. At its peak, your brand becomes a product generator and value creator. This does not happen by accident. Brands must be created and nurtured; brands must be built.

In 1961, the tobacco company RJ Reynolds had reason to feel complacent, smug even. Its market share was approaching 35 percent. It was the dominant force in the American cigarette industry. Among those trailing breathlessly behind—in sixth place—was the Philip Morris company whose market share was less than 10 percent. Executives at RJ Reynolds no doubt sat back in their executive chairs and inhaled deeply one of their successful products. Life is comfortable when you have more than a third of a market in your back pocket.

As the Reynolds executives sat back and contemplated their great success, plans were being hatched at Philip Morris. The company asked ad-man-extraordinaire Leo Burnett to help in repositioning one of its brands aimed at women smokers. On his way from Chicago to a meeting with Philip Morris, Burnett made a few drawings. One of them was of a sheriff smoking Marlboros. Other creatives dreamed up images of men doing rugged work and smoking Marlboros. The idea was born. Jack Landry, the Marlboro brand manager at the time, liked it, and they were in the market with the new campaign.

Later the brand was further transformed. Macho cowboys smoked Marlboros in a mystical place called Marlboro country where the cowboys roamed freely and tumbleweeds rolled. In this vast and romantic land, smokers could truly be themselves. Men *and* women loved it. "In a world that was becoming increasingly complex and frustrating for the ordinary man," Landry explained, "the cowboy represented an antithesis—a man whose environment was simplistic and relatively pressure free. He was his own man in a world he owned."

136

The Marlboro brand imagery created by Leo Burnett in the United States crossed the world and continues to be the cornerstone of the brand's image. All the other elements of Marlboro's marketing follow the essence of this brand. Nancy Brennan Lund, head of marketing at Philip Morris and steward of Marlboro since the late 1980s, is a tough cookie when it comes to protecting the central image of the brand. Quite right.

Marlboro is now more than a U.S. brand. It is an international product, name, and image known the world over. It is the biggest cigarette brand in the world and, according to Interbrand, has a valuation of some $21 billion—even though the number of smokers continues to fall. Its distinctive red and white colors and its advertising featuring romantic images of the classic American cowboy are universal. (In Europe, the only deviation from this has been Marlboro's excursion into Formula 1 auto racing.) Yet, even icons are now facing intensifying competition and competing brands that have little respect for their venerable age and status.

The Thrill of the New

New brands are emerging every day. Think of Zara in retailing; the Korean company, LG, now moving into cell phones and plasma TVs; the Italian jeweler, Bulgari; Hyundai in autos; Novartis in pharmaceuticals; or Lenovo in computing. The brand's the thing and how you leverage your brand is crucial.

Let's step back and get to the basics of brands. The reality is that imitation is the surest way to become an also-ran in the marketplace. So much of business is now about commodities, things that you can get just about anywhere. How many different airlines can get you to Los Angeles? How many different places in your home city sell cups of coffee? How many ways can you ship something overnight? How many places near you sell lumber and nails? How many different kinds of laptops can you buy? The answer, to each of these questions, is (pardon my French) beaucoup! But you will have a different, if not unique, experience if you choose to fly

JetBlue, drink a cup of Starbucks, FedEx that package, repair your outside deck with the help of Home Depot, or boot up a new laptop from Apple. Why so? Well, it's all about the brand each of these companies—and other sweet spot stars—have built. And the word *is* "built."

The title of the book that most needs to be read but hasn't yet been written is *Born to Brand*. It is the branding process that truly separates the vanguard corporations from their anemic brethren. In fact, it recently dawned on me that, if you peruse the names of all the companies heralded in books like *Built to Last* and *Good to Great*, it will quickly become apparent that (as I see it) all of them—all—are the brands of consequence in their chosen industries. Now, that says something. It would appear that some companies (and not others) are *born* to brand themselves uniquely as did the sports legends I just described. So, what is branding all about?

Defining Brands

Let's define some terms. The web site BuildingBrands.com cites a dictionary definition of the term: "a name, sign, or symbol used to identify items or services of the seller(s) and to differentiate them from goods of competitors." Not bad.

In the beginning came the product. Branding was a mark on the product—a signature or symbol—signifying its origin or ownership. The traditional view of what constitutes a brand is summed up by marketing guru Philip Kotler in his classic textbook, *Marketing Management*. Kotler writes: "[A brand name is] a name, term, sign, symbol, or design, or a combination of these, which is intended to identify the goods or services of one group of sellers and differentiate them from those of competitors."[1]

The trouble with older definitions of brands is that they remain preoccupied with the physical product. The product stands alone; the brand exists within corporate ether. The product comes first and the brand does little more than make it clear which company made the product and where. John Pemberton's brain tonic is the product, but the brand—Coca-Cola—is much more.

More recently, and perhaps more usefully, three American consultants have defined branding as "creating a mutually acknowledged relationship between the supplier and buyer that transcends isolated transactions or specific individuals." It is a significant sign of our times that the brand is now pinned around a "relationship" rather than a product.[2]

But, perhaps the most practical and contemporary definition of brands comes from the consultants of Booz Allen Hamilton:

> *Brands are a shorthand way of communicating critical data to the market to influence decisions. Across a multitude of consumer-focused industries, brands are an important means for differentiation and competitive advantage, although they are most influential when customers lack the data to make informed product choices and/or when the differentiation between competitors' versions of the same product are small to non-existent. Additionally, brands take on more significance when consumers place great importance on the decision being made.[3]*

A Brand Is a Bond

I am not the first person to say that a brand is a bond. But I don't think there's anyone on the planet who feels more passionately about that sentiment than I do. To me, the brand of a company is something that summarizes the feelings of the people working there. Are they committed to customers? To quality? To the creation of new and better products and services? To being fiscally responsible? To being honest? To communicating fully and openly? To caring about the planet? You see: Nail the brand of a company and you have started, just by that act, to project the personality of everyone from the CEO to the newest hire. Thus, the brand builds trust between everyone inside the company *and* everyone outside the company: customers, partners, vendors, investors. The brand captures the organizational heart and mind. It is the first step in creating a long and healthy relationship with the customer. To amplify this point, let me bring this to life with three stories I'm fond of.

First, there's a legendary story tied to Akio Morita, one of the founders of Sony. When the company was struggling to get off the ground, Morita was desperate to sell some of Sony's new transistor radios to large buyers, preferably in the United States. Morita picks up the story from there:

> *The people at Bulova liked the radio very much and their purchasing officer said very casually, "We definitely want some of these. We will take one hundred thousand units!" I was stunned. It was an incredible order, worth several times the total capital of our company. We began to talk details, my mind working very fast, when he told me that there was one condition: we would have to put the Bulova name on the radios.*[4]

Guess what? *Morita turned the order down.* He relates in his semi-autobiographical book that the pain of giving up that order was worth it. Morita wanted his products to advance the Sony brand.

I often quote advertising giant David Ogilvy when I talk to groups about branding. Ogilvy said, "A brand is the intangible sum of product attributes." Morita was willing to sell his radio; he just wasn't willing to give away all the intangibles that were already embedded in the newly founded Sony. And that is part of Sony's brand today. Relatedly, Ogilvy & Mather Japan today speaks about *kizuna*, the relationship between products and people. Says the advertising agency: "A brand is a bond between a company, product or service on the one hand and a customer on the other. The main characteristic of this bond is that it is emotional. It is because it is emotional that it can become differentiated, and through differentiation, it creates value."[5]

In the United States, Chick-fil-A continues to reflect the values of its founder, Truett Cathy. Even at age 85, Cathy is still operating the company pretty much as he did when he founded it 60 years ago. You would think that running a $2 billion company operating 1,250 restaurants in 38 states would change things. But, no. Chick-fil-A is true to its sweet spot DNA. Truett believes that Sundays should be days of rest, so none of his stores open on that day.[6] The company's name has become synonymous with its iconic ad campaign. The ads feature cows holding placards urging people to "Eat Mor Chikin."

Woody Faulk, the company's vice president of brand development, sees four ways in which the cow (and the messages accompanying the image) became an icon by helping to symbolize four "emotional connections" with its customers:

1. The first is its "Mom-approved" nutritious and family-friendly menu, which was the first in the United States to introduce fruit bowls for instance.
2. The second factor is its passion for quality, which runs through everything from product development to the service delivery.
3. The third factor is the customer experience, based on the belief that customers prefer fun and interesting interactions.
4. The last factor is the system of core values and beliefs that govern Chick-fil-A's actions: its policy of putting customers first; the importance of working together; the drive to continuously improve; personal excellence; and the duty of stewardship of resources Chick-fil-A possesses.[7]

What I take from this is that Chick-fil-A's brand solidly reflects the DNA of the company and that DNA includes the business genes that look upon its brand as a commitment, a pledge, a personal guarantee that customers attracted to its logo will never be disappointed.

To finish talking about the bond that can exist between products and people, I just have to cite Apple. Scott Bedbury, author of *A New Brand World*, makes an important point about Apple that's worth noting: "Apple wasn't just a protagonist for the computer revolution. Apple was a protagonist for the individual: anyone could be more productive, informed, and contemporary."[8] If Apple ever comes out with a product that belies its brand, it will have broken a bond with its customers, a most sacred bond.

In *The New York Enterprise Report*, David Curtis wrote an elegantly simple (but powerful) digest of what I've been explaining here. In "Building a Brand That Will Build Your Business," he makes the best closing point for this section:

> *A brand is a bond—meaning both a connection and a promise. Therefore, branding is bonding. When you consistently deliver on your brand promise, you strengthen the bond between you and your customers. There are both rational and emotional aspects to the brand bond; but, if anything, how your customers feel about you is more important than what they think about you.*[9]

Misunderstanding Brands

Too many business leaders are lost when it comes to branding. No, they're not lost; they're confused. They think that branding is just marketing (or, worse, advertising) with a capital letter attached to each word. In other words, I have to laugh when a small start-up company (say, the current Silicon Valley overnight wonder) takes millions of its precious start-up funds to advertise during the Super Bowl. They think that will establish them as a new brand, but they are universally disappointed. While *marketing*, the collection and accurate interpretation of data tied to consumer wants and needs, and *advertising*, the broadcasting of an appealing message about a product or service, can fortify a brand, neither of these is branding as people in business need to understand it.

Recognizing that branding is more than marketing and much more than advertising is the starting point for a company destined for sweet spot status. But such a company also realizes that product lines and business units do not, by themselves, a brand make.

But here's the really weird thing. Very few companies understand or apply the power of branding to business-to-business commerce. Think about it. Most companies rely, at some level at least, on selling their goods or services to other companies. Yet, the whole branding effort is focused on consumers. Consider direct marketing, for example, one of many brand-building activities. The reality is that 46 percent of direct marketing—worth some $2.34 trillion—comes from business-to-business companies. Yet, most of the world's marketing is business-to-consumer marketing trying to reach consumers.

Very little marketing is devoted to business-to-business companies. There are very few marketers who devote any time or resources marketing to other companies. This is not because business-to-business does not require marketing but because the companies think very narrowly that marketing can be taken care of through the sales force and distribution channels. They do not try to leverage other aspects of marketing. It is rare to find someone in a business-to-business company who is in charge of the brand. Indeed, most CEOs of these companies do not understand the value of building a strong brand. And most important, they fail to connect the growth strategies of their companies with the brand. Why this is so remains (to me at least) the great marketing mystery. If there is one thing that I have learned it is that business-to-business marketing is a hugely underexploited activity.

Why Brands Matter

Now, just about my entire career has been built on building brands. So I do not speak from theory here; I speak from experience. Starting with the idea that branding is all about "a name, sign, or symbol used to identify items or services of the seller(s) and to differentiate them from goods of competitors," you must first understand why brands matter. Brands matter because internally and externally they give you permission to achieve growth and are one of the main vehicles to make growth a reality.

At Pitney Bowes, coming to grips with the company's branding was at the heart of change. Once we better understood our brand, this effectively gave us permission to explore other adjacent business areas. Customers were more willing to accept the new areas due to the strength of our brand. We heard at numerous focus groups and qualitative studies, Pitney Bowes has been around for 80+ years so we must be doing things right. This is a direct testament to the brand permission.

As I mentioned briefly earlier in this book, when I began working at the company, I brought all the company's marketing material and put it around the walls of a room. One day, we asked the company's top 35 executives to just walk around the room and tell us, in as direct a way as they could, what Pitney Bowes is all about. At the time, the $4 billion company I had just joined was functioning as a $4 million company. Every business group had its own way of doing things. And while that inspires autonomy and entrepreneurship, if it's not managed right, it also splinters the leverage you could have if you united around a single brand.

When I first joined, had I asked any of my fellow executives if Pitney Bowes was a brand-name company, an informed manager or employee, at the time, would have said with precision that Pitney Bowes had 61 different brands. In a nutshell, starting with CEO Mike Critelli, we convinced the top management team that we were wasting a lot of money trying to support 61 brands. In fact, we argued, 61 brands is almost as bad as having *no* brand-name recognition.

As a result, we took 61 brands and considered what to do next. There are three options in this case. First, you can decide that there is one and only one core brand. Think of Dell or BMW. Second, you can have a clearly defined core brand and use flanker brands when strategically required—look at HP, Kraft, and IBM. Or you can have a holding company with disparate brands—a strategy pursued by Procter & Gamble, Philip Morris, and Starwood. We took option two and consolidated our 61 brands into one brand with the option to use flanker brands when needed. We created a decision tree on how the brands could be best consolidated. We looked at how the brands can be migrated over time so that we can still leverage the equity in the old brand and connect it with Pitney Bowes. We created a nomenclature system that is closely aligned with the Pitney Bowes brand and through which we change the names of the existing brands as well as assign names to the new ones. (Now, after a series of acquisitions, the challenge is consolidating names *into* Pitney Bowes.)

Brands Are Bountiful

Converting your business to a brand—or retooling the brand(s) that your company now has—is not something that you should do just to avoid boredom or to impress the board of directors. Brands are bountiful, they grant you permission in all sorts of ways to fully explore your commercial potential.

Jeremy Sampson notes, "Today, brands and other intellectual capital can often make up over 66 percent of the value of a company."[10] The implication (one that I mightily agree with) is that a company that is confused and chaotic in managing its brand (or plugging along with no brand at all) is also slicing and dicing two-thirds of the potential value of the company. Let's hop to Europe. A study by Booz Allen Hamilton of European companies with strong brands provided this fiscal motivation: "80 percent of European companies managed with a strong brand focus have operating profits almost twice as high as the sector average."[11] Do you doubt that statistic would be much different on any other continent? Let me give you my own take on how bountiful a strong brand presence can become for your company.

More than half of a company's market capitalization is based on intangible assets. In every company I have worked in, I have noticed that brand is a *major* driver of the intangible assets. And

145

that's exactly why more and more serious measurements of the impact of brand are being launched.

Little wonder there is a large and growing body of literature on the subject of brand valuation. I'm not going to regurgitate it here. Suffice it to say that success in this area also requires hard work. As David Haigh, chief executive of Brand Finance, has observed:

> We need to acknowledge the difficulty of doing this stuff. One of the problems is that sometimes companies want simple answers when none exist. There is no silver bullet. We must also be careful not to say this is an impossible task so we shouldn't bother. The important point is that we don't let the desire for perfection drive out the good. Financial measures are never perfect. The issue is that marketers have engaged in a meaningful debate, among themselves and with other parts of the business including the board, and come up with the very best measures available.[12]

There are a number of steps to figuring out a brand's worth. First, you have to estimate the revenues that will be generated by the brand over the life of the brand. That means you have to figure out how long you expect a brand to last. The longer it will last, the more it is worth. Next, you have to determine how much you would have to pay a third party to license a comparable brand. This is called the *royalty rate*. Third, you multiply the royalty rate times the annual forecasted revenue of the brand to obtain the *royalty fee*. Of course, you have to pay taxes on that royalty fee. Let's say the tax rate is about 40 percent. So, next, subtract taxes to get your aftertax royalty fee.

But wait a minute. Money you expect to make in future years is not worth as much as money you have in your pocket today. You have to discount money you will earn in the future. So, fifth, you discount the after-tax royalty fees you would pay over time. Then there is one more step. Sixth, you must add together the discounted after-tax royalty fees with certain tax benefits. I won't go into those tax benefits here, but believe me, they exist.

So, reach for the calculator, and you will find that your brand's financial value equals the sum of its forecasted revenue multiplied by what a third party would charge to license a comparable brand, or its "royalty rate." Then you multiply the royalty rate by the annual forecasted revenue of the brand. Then subtract taxes, discount your after-tax royalty fees over time, and add back some tax benefits.

It sounds complicated, I know, so let me show you how it works with Pitney Bowes's brand's value. To establish a royalty rate for Pitney Bowes, the first questions you have to ask are "what and where?" We would have to break the company down into parts, different divisions, and countries such as the United States, Canada, the United Kingdom, Germany, and elsewhere. In some places, like the United States, we have a high penetration rate and are known for our technology. We have high brand recognition. In some foreign countries where we are less active, our brand is not as widely known and our royalty rate would be lower. Let's figure our royalty rate ranges from 1 percent to 8 percent, with the higher rates in the countries where we do the most business. The discount factor would be around 10 percent. From our calculations, our brand would be worth about $3 billion. Not easy, but worthwhile—believe me.

Building Brand

Building Pitney Bowes' brand was not easy or quick. But, looking back, I realize that we did a number of key things—all of which add up to a lesson worth learning. To build one brand, Pitney Bowes:

- Encouraged businesses to start cross-selling.
- Acquired companies that would provide equitable strength throughout our major lines of business.

- Defined what the company stood for after 85 years of doing business—then we started leveraging that well-earned reputation for being trustworthy, having reliable products, and services, and (most of all) providing security for all our customers who entrust their confidential data to our mailing processes.

- Expanded the definition of "who we have been" to "who we are now"—in other words, we started stressing that we weren't just a postage meter company, that we are a high-energy, innovative, dynamic, and confident corporation offering many products and services.

- Promoted a whole new message to the marketplace: that Pitney Bowes is all about helping its customers to create, produce, distribute, and manage their documents; we told the world, loudly, that we were all about "Engineering the flow of communication."

- Took our message and our values to our employees as well: all 35,000 of them in 130 countries were told that we need to start thinking and acting as one company, and we under-pinned that sentiment by stressing our values of offering our customers reliability, trustworthiness, security, and innovativeness.

- Stressed (in workshops, seminars, small-group meetings, newsletters, videos, and teleconferences) that it was now critical for everyone to weigh every action tied to every part of their job to make sure it reflected the new Pitney Bowes; with a newly revised company vision statement, we made sure every employee understood the meaning of the newly added words that defined our company as a global brand.

- Appointed every employee at every level to the status of being a Pitney Bowes Brand Ambassador: We created a one-brand statement, not because we wanted everybody to recite that statement, but because we wanted to help them put their products and services—whatever they did—into the context of the brand.

- Worked very closely with any salesperson or call center staff member to retool themselves in order to speak out our brand through their personal conduct.

- Instituted a brand education program for all the leaders, putting them through a full day of brand education covering topics like identifying your customer, attracting and not repelling your customer, and using our brand to open doors with your customer.

- Created an advertising strategy and program, used direct marketing programs, built an interactive approach, had an events strategy and execution, developed public relations and media relations programs, and community relations programs.

You can see that defining our brand was barely a start at the work that needed to be done. A sweet spot company must use its brand to unify all the distracting or competitive diversity in the company into a unified corporate force.

During all the activities just listed, I personally spoke to 2,000 employees; either one-on-one or via group presentations. The marketing team spoke to more than 20 percent of our employees. That's more than 7,000 people. We told them that uniting behind a single brand is work, hard work—and that there is no shortcut. We asked them to address some very tough internal issues, like the fact that Pitney Bowes at the time had 40 different newsletters for internal employees. So the move to a single brand was a major change for everyone inside the company. But today we're one company with *one* brand. The pay-off is clear and unequivocal: in the past two years alone, Pitney Bowes has grown its own brand equity by 30 percent and we have made substantial improvements against all of our brand attributes.

Brands Are Built

Sweet spot companies use branding in a superior way to achieve superior results. Yet, you would be misled if you thought that branding happens through a curious admixture of serendipity and timing. As I said earlier, putting an advertisement on television during the Super Bowl will put your logo in front of millions of people. But it takes far more than that to actually build a brand. (See Figure 7.1.)

Brand positioning can be complex. You have to look at a number of elements, including: how to make the brand relevant, and differentiated in a way that allows you to expand the brand reach and its credibility. When we introduced the branding campaign at Pitney Bowes, we looked at these criteria to decide on the positioning of the brand. Our positioning of "Engineering the Flow of Communication" and the Mailstream was deeply rooted in making Pitney Bowes more relevant from the customer's standpoint. It

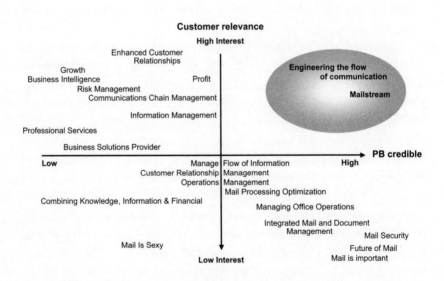

FIGURE 7.1   Pitney Bowes' Positioning Goal: Achieve High Customer Relevance with High Credibility

has the highest credibility; it changes the customer perception and it is differentiated from the competition.

You could look at differentiation, relevance, esteem, and knowledge. Still others might look at presence, relevance, performance, advantage, and bonding. From the customers' standpoint, according to the branding company Landor, differentiation helps in generating trial and repeat purchase; relevance helps in reinforcing choice, and creating relationships; esteem maintains preference and price premium and sustains customer loyalty over time. Knowledge creates active loyalty (brand advocacy), and facilitates the creation of new revenue streams. At the same time, Millward Brown, a marketing research firm, uses a pyramid that helps in developing high loyalty. They start with having presence—to gain some knowledge of the brand. Relevance helps in evoking a set of brand choices. Performance creates the worthiness of consideration. Advantage offers something worthwhile; while bonding helps in getting something unique.

It does not matter whose model you use: The point is that you want to create a bond with customers so that they buy your products and services repeatedly. The key question is will they buy again? Most of the branding world is dependant on this one point. This is also one of the three most important elements in building loyalty besides customer satisfaction and willingness to recommend.

Let me suggest a list of 10 key steps that you will have to take to create a brand for your company. Needless to say, if you feel that your company already has a brand presence, but it isn't working well, this perhaps is a way to retrace your steps in building the brand to see if, perhaps, you missed a step or executed it poorly. Ready? Here are my 10 steps:

1. *To build a brand, you have to start with understanding the DNA of the brand and match it with the DNA of the company.* This is a hard process. Start with assessing the organizational DNA. In other words, try to understand the very essence of the brand. This is the core of the company and/or products and services. Do not try to fake it. You do this by talking to all possible audiences including

customers, employees, investors, regulators, *everyone you can*—and trying to understand the essence of the brand. Then, simultaneously, you have to compare and contrast the perceptions of the marketplace about your company with a rock-hard analysis of how your company really operates. Where the DNA matches, reinforce it. Add staff and budget to maximize the strong points of your company's market position. Where the DNA link is broken between market perception and corporate behavior, it's probably time to change your company in some significant ways.

2. *Branding is essentially a job for those in the marketing function.* But everyone at the top of the company must be integrally involved in any branding effort. In time, as I indicated: Everyone in the company must support the brand. Nonetheless, the second thing I would do is to make sure that the top executive team is overtly connecting the brand building with the company's growth strategy. In other words, it is critical for all those operationally minded executives to realize that branding is not philanthropy; it's about growing the business, increasing revenues, streamlining costs, boosting profits. Don't be afraid to talk about branding with a calculator in your hand.

3. *Focus on what is important.* It's easy when you delve into branding pursuits to start thinking about the minutiae of your business. You could easily wake up in a sweat in the middle of the night and ask, "Gee, I wonder if the small print on Form 1631 reflects the DNA of the company?" You have to keep at the top of your mind that branding is about the big things, first; in most cases, the little things will surely follow. Let it suffice to say that the leaders at Apple were working hard, first, on getting everyone to believe that it was part of the corporate mission to create "insanely great products" before they focused on how they were boxed and wrapped.

4. *Create a brand architecture.* Brands tend to be complex matters. Assuming you are, as I am, a fan of FedEx, try taking this simple examination. In 25 words or less, speak out why you would trust FedEx with your most prized personal possession. See? It's not easy to reduce words like "trust" to a simple statement. Which

152

is why you need to lay out the "architecture" of your brand. Every key component of how you want your company to think, internally, and then relate, externally, to the marketplace needs to be diagrammed as best you can. I am not suggesting a double-tiered 3-D matrix drawn with the best CAD-CAM software your company owns. I am saying that, in Pitney Bowes, we identified the primary pillars of our brand as reliability/trustworthiness/security/innovation. Then, we had to *re*-build our company to make sure those words were never forsaken. Did each of products support those pillars? Did our service systems support those pillars? Did our people, at every level, support those pillars? Did all the ads for all our products support those pillars? Make sure the blueprints for your branding will stand once they are converted into billions of dollars of products and services sold and supported.

5. *Build a brand positioning.* The process just outlined should help in building brand positioning. That means that you have to realize that a brand to attract "everyone" is a poorly-thought-out brand. Instead, make sure your brand correlates to how you've demarcated demand. Look at the Presto! branding done by Nike for its line of clothing products and accessories. What's important, especially if you go to Nike's Presto! web site, is that this line is designed for, aimed at, and built to accommodate people in their 20s.[13] So the site is one of the most nonsalesy web sites you'll find. That is precisely what brand positioning is all about. You have to think about the (a) values, (b) subjective benefit, (c) objective benefit, and (d) attributes that you're trying to link to the marketplace via your branding effort. Chick-fil-A's cow is not for fine diners. Apple never has been about attracting chief information officers. And when Home Depot says, "You can do it. We can help," they are not aiming that message at professional contractors.

6. *Verify your brand personality.* Some 10 years ago, David Aaker wrote *Building Strong Brands*, and there are many reasons why that book has endured for so long.[14] Aaker is especially enlightening on making sure you think about your brand as a living presence. By doing this, you start to realize that—just like different

people—brands can have different personalities. Aaker offers some interesting choices. Does your brand (do you *want* your brand to) come across as: Down-to-earth, family oriented, genuine, old-fashioned? Spirited, young, up-to-date, outgoing? Accomplished, influential, competent? Pretentious, wealthy, condescending? Athletic and outdoorsy?[15] In sum, Aaker suggests (and I want to echo this, loudly) that you should ask: "What if the brand spoke to you?" You need to make sure that your brand is speaking with a tone that is proper for your targeted market.

7. *Establish long-lasting emotional ties with customers and prospects.* I realize this could sound like a command that is easy to say and hard to do, like "go make a friend" or "learn to dance." I don't mean it so. It's just that there is a fundamental flaw in so many branding efforts that I've watched collapse over the years. Remember when banks said they wanted to be "your personal banker"? Those campaigns ended when customer after customer was summarily dismissed the very second that the teller at the window finished the transaction. I heard some years back that even McDonald's realized it had to work on its employees who were serving the same repeat customers *every day* and yet did not make any effort to get to know their names. In other words, there is a set of priorities that you must put into place—operational priorities—that underscore to employee and customer alike that your brand is not about a one-time sale; it's about helping customers for life. To the extent that you learn about your customers, that you database what you've learned, and that you act on the data in your hands, you will either build a long-term relationship or snap it. Next time you go to a Starbucks, see if *anyone* behind the counter acts like this is the last cup of coffee they are selling to each customer in line. No way. Not at Starbucks. At least, not at Starbucks when it operates the way Howard Schultz would have it. Each cup of coffee served, he would say, should be an invitation to have another cup as soon as you can return.

8. *Create a timeless and valuable value proposition.* This is an especially important point to check. Customers are not naïve and they are not dumb. Increasingly, they measure every vendor (every

vendor!) by their own standards of value. So, you can have the most memorable and magnetic branding; but if a customer senses, in the end, that they are being gouged for the goods or services you provided, they will abandon the long-term relationship that you so desperately want to create. I had a friend tell me recently that he called Amazon customer service to see if they would price-match an external hard disk. The answer from Amazon: They don't price match. But, the customer service agent was quick to point out, Amazon.com stands behind every product it sells, wants to make sure you get exactly what you want, and (via a new program just introduced) will fast-ship a customer's order at low or no cost. Called "Amazon Prime," there is an annual fee to get that service, but it can save a loyal Amazon customer many dollars if he or she buys frequently. In sum, Amazon may not always have the lowest price on the Internet, but it has worked hard to make sure it has one of the best value propositions.

9. *Develop a vision consistent with your branding by incorporating your values and operating principles in your brand. Then, make that vision pervasive in your organization. Make sure everyone becomes a Brand Ambassador.* The term "brand ambassador" will bring up lots of hits on Google; it's not a new concept. But I'd like to add a dimension to the term you may not have given much thought to. If today, the president of the United States appointed *you* to be ambassador to another country, my guess is that you would be stunned, then delighted, then terrified. The terror in the appointment would come from the fact that you, more than likely, don't know the U.S. position on dealing with the country you are about to move to. It's the same in business. Starting at the top, the company must have a brand that mirrors its vision of what the company should be all about and it must have brand ambassadors acting as evangelists for the brand and what it stands for.

10. *Connect your brand to all the key company touchpoints: advertising, public relations, web site, internal communications, investor communications—all your communications.* In my experience, surprisingly few companies leverage their brand with investor communication. Make sure that your annual report and other

investor communications are closely linked to the brand. I list this item as the last of 10 steps not because it's less important or because it's "icing on the branding cake." This is an important, even crucial, step. Once you know your brand in all the other dimensions listed earlier, you must make sure that some stray communication doesn't confuse anyone, especially customers. I call all these communication conduits "touchpoints." That's because, when you or someone else in the company isn't able to be face-to-face with a customer, a vendor, or an investor, the way such people gauge the company's brand is by something visual or verbal on paper or on an electronic screen. Thus, it is worth an enormous effort to make sure that you are not inadvertently saying one thing via your brand and another thing via your publications. "Walking the talk" usually refers to what a person does or doesn't do in terms of exhibiting the values of a company. Know what? The same principle applies to published information. It's amazing how easy it is for a company to have a brand that's built on warm rapport with customers and yet also have a web site that is cold and sterile, hard to use, slow, and not up-to-date. Beware!

Expand Your Brandwidth

Branding is not an initiative; it does not start and then end. It is a way of life. It's the way you live the brand. So, you have to start, and you have to keep nurturing it. It's a living and breathing thing. You have to keep feeding it, and you have to keep changing it as you go along.

What you have to do, perhaps before anything else, is find the brand DNA. When all is said and done, this DNA is quite simply *what is of paramount importance to your company*. You absolutely have to dig, dig, and yet dig harder to find that DNA. Your company may be so large that it needs multiple brands. Perhaps that's true. But I have learned that, when brands multiply, they can counteract each other much more easily than they can complement each other. So, tread gently in creating multiple brands.

In the case of the branding episodes within Pitney Bowes, we discovered that, basically, we do two things for our living having to do with mail and other forms of communication. That said, we help people boost their efficiency; and, thus, we help them to become more effective. Those are the two most important things that we do. We thus had the two most important links to our DNA and to our emerging brand.

There are different ways to connect those two things to all our products, services, and people. Some of these ways are better than others. Fair enough; but in the last analysis, branding is pointless if you don't connect it to your company, its customers, and your growth strategy. Consciously. Consistently. Completely. "Generating growth while maintaining the consistency of brand is very hard. The two elements, constant growth and consistency are hard to achieve," admits Mike Linton, CMO of Best Buy.

You start with the DNA umbrella and then have each line of business in your company—and all the others who support your lines of business—ask: "How do we really make that umbrella meaningful to our line of business?" If you do not do that, if you do not connect your branding in just that way, then it will wither and die. It will become "just another corporate program" and you might as well retire no matter how young you are.

But let's not close on a downer. Branding is perhaps the most powerful way to connect your company to its chosen marketplace. When it's done right, it creates the economic rationale for customers to keep coming back for more. Happily. And, done right, it can help you define in much more detailed and exciting ways what your customers want from your company. That can spell innovation in your operating systems but, much more likely, in your product line. An added, but not to be underestimated plus point of brands, is that they build confidence within your company. People want to feel proud and a great brand gives them something to believe in and to be proud of.

Apple CEO Steve Jobs was interviewed by NBC anchorman Brian Williams. The reason was the opening of a new Apple Store right on Fifth Avenue. It's a glass cube, and even the pictures of the store are titillating.[16] But Brian Williams's interview went beyond the store's architecture to ask Jobs about his own mental architecture. He asked if it was reasonable to be running a company where, every time a new product is introduced, it's overshadowed by the next big breakthrough introduced in only a few months. Jobs didn't blink.

He replied that Apple knows its customers, and its customers know Apple. Given that, it has built a brand that keeps both the marketplace and Apple Computer charged up at the same time. Jobs asserted that the loyalty of people to the Apple brand mandates that it keeps coming out with a new iPod every year or so. And Jobs said to NBC's top newsman that Apple's customers relish the chance to keep coming back, year after year, to buy the latest technology. Jobs implied that Apple's customers would be disappointed if he didn't give them the chance. Now that's brandwidth!

Sweet Spotter: Zara

The fashion retailer Zara is a brand you will be hearing much more from in the years ahead, especially if you reside in the United States. Elsewhere, you may already have been to a Zara store. They are exciting places—and I say that as a 40-something year-old man with only a passing interest in the world of fashion. Take it from me, they buzz. Why?

They Invented Techno-Fashion

Zara began as a small lingerie company, based in La Coruna, Spain. How did it grow into an enterprise that has 760 women's clothing stores in 55 countries? When CNN profiled the company in 2004, here was the answer given: "The secret, according to CEO Jose Castellano, is its reliance on communication, and the way it uses existing technology to take control of almost every aspect of design, production, and distribution."[17]

Zara is into "cheap chic" or "disposable fashion." *Fortune* did a nice job of capturing the allure of the company; just consider its lead in describing the power of this company:

> *Long before the new economy made catchwords of speed, customization, supply-chain management, and information sharing, Spanish clothing retailer Zara was carrying out a revolution of its own. By translating the latest trends into designs that are manufactured in less than 15 days—and delivering them to its stores twice a week— Zara pioneered a new kind of quick, custom-made retailing that has transformed the relatively low-profile retailer into a global powerhouse. "Nobody else can get new designs to stores as quickly," says Keith Wills, European-retail analyst at Goldman Sachs. "Unless you can do that, you won't be in business in 10 years."[18]*

They Linked Their Customers Right to Headquarters

But as revolutionary as Zara is, its business model is basic-basic-basic. Simply put, Zara linked the small-store dynamic (the shopkeeper serving the daily desires and whims of his best customers, religiously) with the enormous scale of global enterprise (via seamless communications). As *Fortune* points out, all of Zara's stores are patched into a single, real-time communications network so that its headquarters in Spain can react and respond to customers *just like that:*

Store managers monitor how merchandise is selling and transmit this information, as well as customer requests, to headquarters. "The role of the store manager goes way beyond that of Gap and H&M [Hennes & Mauritz]," says [Keith] Wills of Goldman Sachs. Together with trend-spotters who travel the globe in search of new fashion, store managers make sure their designers have access to real-time information when deciding with the commercial team on the fabric, cut, and price points of a new garment.[19]

Zara's designers come up with some 40,000 new creations every year; about 10,000 go into production and then into stores. Zara's customers have learned that, if they're not there fast—when the new products come in, then there's a good chance they will miss the opportunity to buy "the latest fashion," literally. Then again, those who snap up the latest usually wear it right away, without fearing that the same outfit will appear on all their friends.

BusinessWeek certainly thinks that Zara is working a special kind of sweet spot magic. And the publication notes that Zara is no test bed concept. Zara isn't some professor's model; it's a BIG business. Technically, Zara is part of Industria de Diseño Textil (also known as Inditex). In fact, Zara is the flagship of Inditex, which saw its 2005 sales up 21 percent. Zara-Inditex is an $8.15 billion business[20] with 60,000 employees worldwide.[21] And the reason you will be hearing much more about Zara in the United States is that the nascent fast-fashion business accounted for a skimpy 1 percent of the U.S. clothing market in 2005 (and Zara's only a fraction of that 1 percent). As *BusinessWeek* succinctly put it, Zara has "plenty of room to grow."[22]

They Are Open for Business—And Totally Open!

I'm not sure how many companies are as open and accessible as Zara. You can even download their business model![23] Zara's strength is not in its blueprint for success; it's in its execution of its blueprint. That's its competitive edge. And that execution plainly comes from 60,000 employees taught to work seamlessly in pursuit of the brand strategy communicated heartily by its top executives. Its current CEO, Pablo Isla Álvarez de Tejera, is an easy presence to find on any Internet search, which reveals he is the globetrotter you would expect. And, as with the brand itself, you should be hearing a lot more from Zara and its CEO. The chain plans to open 40 stores in the United States by 2008.[24]

8

Champions-In-Chief

Sweet Spot Skill #4: Make your top executives the first new members of the marketing department. It's a good thing if your C-suite residents become overtly identified with your company's product line. Are your top executives on a campaign?

When I was working with Ford, customer segmentation, market assessment, product availability, and competitive landscape analysis were just the beginning of the program. The harder challenge was how to convince management, particularly the U.S. car designers, that they needed to focus on a global concept. The other challenge was to persuade American management to accept the prospect that a successful midsize car design could come from Europe.

In the decisive meeting with top executives, we started with a presentation to Don Petersen, chairman of Ford Motor Company, and his direct reports. We prepared a slide presentation with the consumer story well laid out and added our recommendations from the six months of lifestyle research we had already done in Europe and North America. The research was called 4Cs—*Cross Cultural Consumer Characterization*—and it was the brainchild of Satish Korde (now head of the Ford Motor Company Group at WPP Group). Satish also led the work to understand consumers globally.

Let me set the scene. The boardroom at Ford's world headquarters is a staid, wood-paneled affair that can intimidate even the best of presenters. You can sniff the history and always suspect that Henry Ford himself is going to walk through the door and announce that your presentation is baloney. Don walked in with some of his direct reports. He was sitting in the middle and his direct reports were seated next to him on both sides. Mentally, we were speculating on the people who would support our perspective on how to change the strategy of Ford Motor Company; but, most important, we also wanted to know the blockers, the ones who might not be supportive of the recommendation and who, in fact, might try to keep anything new from happening.

There were many "biggies" in attendance besides Ford's CEO. In the room was Bob Rewey, the head of North American operations, who had just come back from a stint in the United Kingdom as chairman of Ford's European operations, as well as Edsel Ford, son of Henry Ford II, the modern patriarch who brought Ford Motor Company from the brink of bankruptcy. Edsel, who had learned the automotive business in the lap of his father, was the general marketing manager of Lincoln Mercury division, and was also our immediate client for Young & Rubicam. But there were many others confronting us as well, including those who were the chiefs of design for Ford's product line.

On the heels of a major success resulting from the introduction of the company's first "aerodynamic" cars, Ford was riding quite high. Before that the automotive industry worldwide had only "boxy" cars. Aerodynamic design was a huge investment for Ford. Some estimated that the company had spent upward of $5 billion on the platform of Taurus and Sable. The shape of the cars was controversial (some said it was a jelly bean design), but the marketing types termed them aerodynamic cars. We leveraged the new design and showcased it in all advertising. We created a new spot with the music of a current pop music diva ("Do you want to dance?") and showed the Mercury Sable appearing to dance. Mercury's tag line was "the shape you want to be in."

We were well on our way to a successful launch of Mercury Sable, but, admittedly, it was going to be hard to win over everyone. Many of the upper Midwest execs seemed to think that all cars should be designed with a Detroit frame of mind. We wanted a Euro-based design approach, and we were arguing for the ditching of two cars now in Ford's showrooms: Tempo and Topaz. It was a stretch for some of these execs to think that a car could be created with a team of designers from the United States *and* from the United Kingdom and Germany, but we had one major argument going for us: We knew from months of research what the customer wanted. And, in the end, that rationale prevailed.

What I learned from this was simple: *Understand customers.* Dig deep into the marketplace. And connect all that knowledge to the very top of the company. Without C-suite buy-in and active support, any marketing idea or strategy is dead in the water. The C-suite has to be your champions-in-chief.

Hit the Road

It's not because they're extroverts. Or because they love the spotlight, applause, or adulation. And it's not because they are trying to rack up frequent flier miles. No, whenever you see and hear a CEO of a small, or lesser known, business barnstorming the globe—meeting with customers, speaking at conferences, appearing on television interviews, shaking hands with his or her employees—it's because this leader realizes that the last place he or she needs to be is behind a desk. One CEO told me that when he got his job, he hit the road. He was hardly ever in his freshly decorated corner office. After a few months, the chairman called him over after a meeting. "Is there something wrong?" he asked "People are noticing that you're never here." The CEO's reply was as blunt as it is true: "There aren't any customers in my office. That's where I am—meeting customers." A sweet spot company gets to that status for a lot of good reasons, but it's almost impossible for any enterprise to catapult to the top of the list of marketplace masters unless the CEO is willing to lead the charge.

Now, there are lots of ways to lead the corporate charge. Some CEOs I have worked with have tended to tell people what to do and to expect the C-suite to follow dutifully in line. If it works, don't knock it. Others are consensus builders. The change they initiate takes longer to reach fruition, but it is sustainable.

Let me take you back to a time you probably don't think about much, the past. For this exercise, I want you to try to pretend that you don't know the names of Wal-Mart, or Panasonic, or Southwest Airlines. That's *hard*, isn't it!

But stay with me on this; you'll get the point—and soon.

On the Road with Sam

It's very early in the 1990s, and Wal-Mart is starting to catch widespread attention (translation: a feature story in *Fortune*). And what is it that people are reading about the company that is challenging Sears, Roebuck and all other comers? More important, what are they reading about the founder of Wal-Mart, Sam Walton? Well. . . .

- That Walton has made a pledge to visit every Wal-Mart store at least once every year; with 365 days on the calendar, Walton realizes that this is going to be hard. There are already 1,650 stores and 250 related Sam's Clubs—and the company is opening an average of three new stores *every week*.

- That Walton is far from "encumbered" by this task. He says, "This is still the most important thing I do, going around to the stores, and I'd rather do it than anything I know of. I know I'm helping our folks when I get out to the stores. I learn a lot about who's doing good things in the office, and I also see things that need fixing, and I help fix them. Any good management person in retail has got to do what I do in order to keep his finger on what's going on. You've got to have the right chemistry and the right attitude on the part of the folks who deal with the customers."

- That, when he visited the largest store in the Memphis area, he called all the employees up front and told them that he was impressed *that the floor was so clean!* Walton asks everyone to sit down, then says, "This floor is so clean— let's sit down on it. [Everyone sits, and Sam crouches on one knee, like a coach designing a play in overtime.] I thank you. The company is so proud of you, we can hardly stand it."

- That Walton is not just doing all this to make him "one of the boys" or to offer up token words of gratitude from a distant and aloof chief executive. Nope. Walton continues, "But you know, that confounded Kmart is getting better, and so is Target. So what's our challenge? Customer service, that's right. Are you thinking about doing those extra little things? Are you looking the customer in the eye and offering to help? You know, you're the real reason for Wal-Mart's success. If you don't care about your store and your customers, it won't work. They like the quality and they like the attitude here. They like that we save 'em money, don't they? And they say, 'Hey, something's different about Wal-Mart.'"

Different, indeed. And while all of this came from a *Fortune* feature story by John Huey, at the time relatively little was known about Walton, other than that his stores were racking up impressive sales and his employees seemed to be his biggest fans.[1]

An Important Announcement

Let's talk Panasonic. Today, it's probable that you've at least heard of Konosuke Matsushita, the founder of the corporation that now bears his name. Panasonic, of course, is the brand we all know. But in 1932, who knew either of them? Matsushita was, as you might have guessed, the typical entrepreneur. He worked for a small company that did not appreciate his inventiveness, so he created his own enterprise. Yawn. But wait. Almost from the very beginning, Matsushita was not in any way the typical start-up CEO, pushing for an ever-growing list of new products while also pushing, pushing, pushing for cash flow—and profits. Harvard's John Kotter is the professor who has done the most to capture the legacy and management philosophy of Matsushita and who wrote *Matsushita Leadership*.[2]

Kotter tells the story of how Matsushita (in 1932) called all his employees together one day and announced that the company's mission, from that point forward, was to produce high-quality electronic goods that would be so inexpensive that their benefits would be available to everyone, worldwide. "Our mission as a manufacturer is to create material abundance by providing goods as plentifully and inexpensively as tap water," Matsushita said, "This is how we can banish poverty, bring happiness to people's lives, and make this world a better place."[3]

Okay, nice *talk*. But as Kotter points out, Matsushita immediately reorganized the company into three divisions (in essence, small business units) and made each one autonomous, responsible for its share of the 200 products now being made somewhere inside the growing enterprise. Two years later, he created an Employee Training Institute to teach, among other things, his own values and priorities as a CEO. And he was involved in employee education from that point forward. And why, with all the demands placed on any CEO, then or now, did he dedicate so much time to this? It was for the customer, the only one who could take this still-growing company and make it into an international brand. He knew that his place was, first, with his own employees and then with his customer base. It was his most important job. As he said at one time, "Better service for the customer is for the good of the public, and this is the true purpose of enterprise."[4]

Getting "Out There"

Herb Kelleher is the most recent example I can cite of an "historical" CEO who seemed to be tirelessly *out there* promoting his company and his brand. We've all heard (perhaps too much) about the fun-loving culture of Southwest Airlines. But, it is something—in that industry—to have some three decades, straight, of profitable growth. And, to be sure, there are many reasons for this success. But let's not discount the role of this CEO in the equation. As one article noted: "The key to Southwest's success is largely thought to be the warmth and determination of its employees who mirror those same qualities in their leader."[5] The ongoing success of Wal-Mart and Panasonic—*and Southwest*—testifies to Kelleher's endurable presence. But that's the assessment today; what is it that Kelleher did *back then*, when the company was trying to grab a sustainable spot in the merciless airline business?

There are many accounts of this CEO who virtually crusaded both inside and outside the company for recognition of what was unique about Southwest and its own brand of flying. For example:

- One customer said that, over 10 years, he sat next to Kelleher on a number of flights; and each time, the customer was grilled by the CEO on how the airline was doing.[6]

- Kelleher made it clear that he considered himself not just a CEO but a marketing officer: "We market ourselves based on the personality and spirit of ourselves. That sounds like an easy claim but, in fact, it is a supremely dangerous position to stake out because if you're wrong, customers will let you know—with a vengeance. Customers are like a force of nature: You can't fool them, and you ignore them at your own peril."

- Kelleher did all this via a rigorous schedule of meeting with employees and making clear what the airline was all about. And what was his message, in employee meeting after employee meeting? This stands out for me: "The intangibles are more important than the tangibles. Another airline can go out and get airplanes. They can acquire ticket counter space at the terminal. They can buy baggage conveyors and tugs. But the hardest thing for a competitor to imitate—in the customer service business, at least—is attitude; *esprit de corps* is the way that you treat customers and the way that you feel about people. And it's very difficult to emulate that, because you can't do it mechanically, and you can't do it programmatically, and you can't do it according to a formula."[7]

I recall hearing the story (and I have no doubt it's true) that a group of Southwest employees once grumbled that, being third-shift workers, they couldn't meet with Kelleher in person. Upon hearing this, what did Kelleher do? He immediately scheduled a Question & Answer session with them to be held on "their time," in the middle of the night.

Now, there are two ways to look at people like Walton, Matsushita, and Kelleher. You could argue that these are unique personalities—call them extremely social or call them "hams"—and that, unless you have the same DNA, there's really very little to learn from them. That, in my judgment, would be a huge mistake. As I've studied sweet spot companies, it is uncanny how the C-suite executives (Note: I am talking about more than just the CEO!) are willing and able to play the role of "chief marketing officer" any time and anywhere. They are *out there*—with customers, with stockholders, with the press, with subcontractors, vendors, and (most of all) with their employees.

The C-Suite Must Love Consumers

It makes me cry. I have seen so many companies that have executive chiefs who seem to think that their job is all-inside; and not only do they stay principally inside their company walls, they stay *inside their offices*. I have come to see such companies as completely missing the leadership genes required to make them sweet spot candidates. And I increasingly advocate the wisdom in the rule (first devised, I believe, by Sam Walton) that executives should never be allowed to stay more than two days in a row at corporate headquarters.

"If your CEO thinks about customers, it is easy for the marketing team," Wal-Mart chief marketer John Fleming told me. The crucial word is *think*. CEOs who actually put themselves in the place of consumers are rare indeed. Beware of the CEO who has a conversation with a single consumer and reaches conclusions based on that single interaction. It happens. I worked on the development of an ad with a $4 million production cost. Then the CEO happened to outline the campaign and the song we were planning to use to his neighbor. She strongly disapproved of our planned

171

use of the word "devil." The campaign was pulled on the opinion of someone over a garden fence.

Howard Schultz, Starbucks' CEO, visits 30 to 40 of his stores every week not only in order to take the pulse of the customers but also to spread his unique gospel of how to run a business. Schultz says, "I need to touch as many people as possible—I want to spend time with people," he says. "That's the single most important thing I'm doing."[8] It's not just a coincidence that spending time with people is a major part of what Starbucks is all about. Of course, there's the coffee. And the sandwiches. And the desserts. But for a company that avers that its purpose is to "balance being a competitive leader and being a benevolent employer," Schultz and his other top executives are models for far more than coffee consumption— and that perhaps explains why there's no better salesman for Starbucks than Schultz himself. Is it any wonder that Schultz was cover-story content for *BusinessWeek?* Titled "Starbucks' Secret Ingredient," it was the subtitle for the news story that told it all: "How you can incorporate coffee chain chairman Howard Schultz' persuasive communication skills in your workplace."[9]

Advocates in Chief

I've noted that Steve Jobs, of Apple, regularly speaks and makes appearances on behalf of his company. Sweet spot companies are led by CEOs and other C-suite officers who believe so strongly in the company's wares that it's unacceptable to sit back and let others spread the news. The top leaders in sweet spot companies are exuberant proponents of the brand they built.

A speech by Fred Smith of FedEx is a pleasure to attend, but it's not by any means a rarity. Then again, it says something when the chief economist for FedEx, Dr. Gene Huang, is, in an indirect but effective way, making his own pitch for the company.[10] Even Howard Schultz has been outflanked by his energetic CEO, Jim Donald. One newspaper report quoted Schultz as saying that no one keeps the pace of public appearances that Donald does: "I'm only six months older than he is, but I don't have the stamina that he has, candidly," said Schultz, describing a recent whirlwind European tour in which Donald maintained a dawn-to-midnight schedule while all his companions faltered with fatigue. "I could not stay with him," said Schultz.[11]

At Pitney Bowes, Mike Critelli is highly active in influencing postal regulation—which affects our business—across the world. He is also highly active on the Hill ensuring that U.S. postal regulations fit the economic reality we see every day in the mail marketplace. We try to place our top executives in front of customers as often as possible; we really demand that the top 100 leaders in our company perform this task. And when one of our top executives makes a public appearance, we try to capture it on video or audio and place it on our web site. We even have a matrix to decide who goes out to face the media on a certain topic.[12] This is all about C-suite alignment. Everyone on the same team needs to have the same hymn sheet in front of them. (See Figure 8.1.)

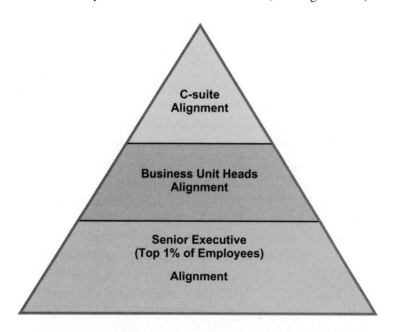

FIGURE 8.1 C-suite Alignment

The most interesting exercise we did in this regard was some-thing I've not heard any other company do. We held a two-day con-ference with our top 200 leaders. At the end of the first day of the meeting, we broke the leaders into about 10 different groups, saying to each group: "Here is a video camera and any items that you need. Go out and create commercials stressing what Pitney Bowes is all about, directed at a specific audience." Almost every group com-plained that "we didn't know that advertising was so hard!" Welcome to marketing. Yet the value of the exercise was substantial; that exer-cise really got them involved in thinking about the customer and how they are going to talk to their customers. On the second day of the conference, we showed the commercials. What you're probably thinking is quite correct: We never ran those commercials publicly because some of them were great and others I'm still not so sure about. That single exercise, however, brought the company together, starting with the top 200 leaders, who now know that they are, *and must always be*, part of the Pitney Bowes marketing team.

CEOs—In Playboy?

The founders of Google, Larry Page and Sergey Brin, are such forceful public advocates that there's even a pretend blog that par-odies what they might say if indeed they used such a communica-tions tool.[13] It's all Internet fun, but the real point is that Page and Brin *are* champions. To begin with, how many CEOs would agree to an interview in *Playboy?* (And how many CEOs would *Playboy* invite to be interviewed?)[14] Read the interview and there's little about lust and a lot about the underlying belief system of Page and Brin—how they did not want Google to ever forget the imperative to "not be evil." Without any doubt, you get the immediate feel-ing that these two billionaire gentlemen aren't shy about their points of view nor restricted to a single-minded goal of just mak-ing money. Google is trying to become an icon for good.

It would be easy to misread my belief that sweet spot com-panies need champions-in-chief. Please know that I am *not* speaking about senior officers of a company taking words scripted by wordsmiths in the bowels of the marketing organization and then going out to mouth these words, with a smile and quick shuffle. That not only would be insincere, it would quickly become the stuff of ridicule. What I am talking about is every single member of the C-suite being an evangelist for the company. Evangelism is teamwork. Think of Ray Ozzie, Bill Gates, and Steve Ballmer at Microsoft—the ultimate tag team.

Understand Consumers; Understand Marketing

If the C-suite understands consumers, it is the first step to understanding marketing. To lead growth, CEOs must understand marketing. Growth is marketing's *raison d'etre*. That's where the trouble begins. Most CEOs do not understand the value of building a strong brand. And, most important, they fail to connect the growth strategies of their companies with the brand. This is a crucial oversight and one that is costing corporate America billions of dollars in missed opportunities. "CEOs already see that their most important challenges are marketing ones—they just don't believe that marketers themselves can confront them," observes Professor Nirmalya Kumar of London Business School.

Marketers need to take charge and educate the C-suite on the value of marketing. The key person, obviously, is the CEO. We are especially fortunate at Pitney Bowes that Chairman and CEO Mike Critelli really understands the value of building a brand, and he has been a steadfast supporter of marketing when it comes to building long-term value. If you boil down the CEO's job, it is focused on creating three types of value: shareholder value (owned by finance), customer value (owned by marketing), and employee value (owned by human resources).

Marketing needs to own the customer value part of the equation completely. We need to build a good customer value proposition that results in meeting the wants and needs of the customers.

We need to get out of the comfort zone of building just the best marketing communication and venture into the world of creating growth strategy that is deeply rooted in customer insights. Once marketing steps up to this challenge, the CEO will take notice.

This is happening in some companies. General Electric CEO Jeff Immelt has stated that "sophisticated marketing" is now one of the company's three imperatives, along with risk taking and innovation. "Jeff has launched us on a journey to become one of the best sales and marketing companies in the world," says David R. Nissen, CEO of GE Consumer Finance.

The Value of CMOs

And yet, marketing representatives are notably absent from the C-suite. How many companies have a chief marketing officer (CMO)? Not many. And when they do have CMOs they tend not to last very long. Research by the headhunters Spencer Stuart found that the average tenure of CMOs was less than 23 months and 86 percent of CMOs had been with their companies for less than three years.

Why? Because most get sucked into marketing communications. If you're still thinking like a marketing communications person, then you're dead. The average tenure of a CEO is four years. So most CEOs will see *two* CMOs come and go.

Insight into the pressures faced comes from Mike Linton, CMO of Best Buy. "We manage three things, it is like a triangle: the company's expectation, innovation, and the business operating model. My role is to keep a balance between short-term and long-term objectives; and between established and new tools," says Mike. "There are so many things going on both short term and long term that if something doesn't go well, it can knock you off very easily. This is one of the reason why CMO tenure is so limited. As a CMO, prioritization becomes your best friend. We get so much from the public, we have to make many choices that are highly visible that require tremendous amounts of objectivity."

The first thing that must happen in the C-suite is for the role of the CMO to be clarified. The CMO's role is to differentiate the company and its products and services from the competition and to propel growth for the company. The risk is that the CMO begins to focus on other things. It is not only that marketing tends not to be championed at board level. Too often, marketing and finance have a relationship of mutual suspicion. Finance regards marketing as a perennial corporate beggar: Give them a few cents and they'll spend it on the corporate equivalent of moonshine and all you're left with is a hangover. Marketers tend to regard the finance department as penny pinchers with little idea of what goes on in the real world of the marketplace. The reality is that there is a natural convergence for the CFO with the CMO—financial/competitive intelligence; acquisitions; investor communications. Traditionally the two have been poles apart, but recent changes in accounting rules for acquisitions will force the CFO and CMO to work together.

Many of the same problems occur in other business functions. The chief information officer (CIO) also needs to be a marketer. Marketing now requires greater accountability. Fortunately, there are more tools and technology available to assess the impact of the marketing program. In addition, the rise in multichannel marketing makes it even more critical to design programs that can test marketing's effectiveness. And testing requires extensive database management. Information technology inside any company is responsible for investing in the infrastructure of the technology that can assess the effectiveness of marketing.

And then there are people. As marketing has become increasingly complicated, it requires constant support from employees to deliver products and services as promised. The customer experience has become paramount. The customer experience is delivered by each and every employee.

This is even more important in a business-to-business company in which the employees are critical in delivering the services. The CMO needs to have a very close relationship with the human resources department so that they can help in training the employees in the brand experience. In summary, CMOs need to be better connected across the enterprise to set the path for growth of a company.

Making Marketing Meaningful

It may help you to grasp the importance of C-suite buy-in to think of the importance of one word that emanates from the sales and marketing world but that has a connotation your top executives should understand. That word is *campaign*. If there is one thing I've noted about sweet spot companies, it's that they are on a mission, they are driving, they are as intent on winning customers as England soccer star Wayne Rooney is intent on scoring soccer goals or as Serena Williams is intent on winning tennis sets. So, what exactly is the rationale for these two starting points for C-suite buy-in? Let's propose and explain at the same time.

You Can't Blow an Uncertain Trumpet

It was Theodore Hesburg, an early president of Notre Dame, who claimed that "The very essence of leadership is that you have to have a vision. It's got to be a vision you articulate profoundly on every occasion. You can't blow an uncertain trumpet."[15] I love that phrase. And I find it most easy to insinuate its import into the business world.

Whatever your product or service, the CEO must be the person leading the charge for the brand of company you have chosen to be. And the value of knowing this is more than the obvious. Would people have screamed if Sam Walton shopped at Kmart or if Konosuke Matsushita was seen playing a Sony radio? Yes. But what's really at stake is the public perception (and by that I mean people both inside and outside the company) that the CEO and the other top officers of any company believe deeply, firmly, and truly in what their company has to offer the public. At Pitney Bowes, Mike Critelli knows our products inside out. He even has six patents registered under his own name.

Every CEO needs to be as fluent in the company's product line as the salesforce. I am not suggesting that Don Petersen, back when he was CEO of Ford, had to be able to cite the tech specs on every vehicle in the product line. But he had to be able to give a stump speech at any time and at any place on the vision and values of Ford—and how they are translated into Ford's products and services—that was an absolute requirement. Petersen, in fact, did this quite well; William Ford, the company's current CEO, is being held to the same standard. And the CEO of your company is as well. Ditto, to my mind, the chief operations officer, the chief information officer, the chief of human resources, and on and on.

Lord John Browne, the chief of British Petroleum, argues that one reason why big businesses are often held in such low regard is that they are not overt in talking about what they do and why they do it. In his own words, he argues that top corporate officers must get "out there" as a first responsibility of their work:

> Responsibility is not something outside the process of doing good business. It is absolutely integral to everything we do. Our commitment to responsibility has to be expressed not in words, but in the actions of the business, day-in and day-out, in every piece of activity, and every aspect of behavior. The common picture—of amoral business requiring constraint—misses the point. Good business should generate a profit by satisfying human needs, and it should do this in a way that is sustainable. And it should contribute to the lives and progress of individuals—giving them opportunity in ways that no other element of society can offer.[16]

To Trust You, They Have to Know You

Throughout this chapter, I have been focusing on CEOs and other top officers leaving the confines of their C-suite offices and getting "out there" to campaign for what they believe and what the company manufactures or provides to the public as a result. In some cases, I have stressed the importance of C-suite executives also connecting regularly with the company's employees. Which is more important? The answer is *both*. And the reason for this is *trust*.

It's hard to remember when the once-mighty IBM was diving in the marketplace. Its computers were too big; its operating system too clumsy; its sales tactics too starchy; its sales numbers too meager; its stock price too low. The CEO who had to fix the problems was Lou Gerstner Jr., the first CEO in the history of the company who came from outside IBM. And Gerstner indeed turned IBM around; but it's no accident that, in his memoir about the challenges he faced *(Who Says Elephants Can't Dance?)*,[17] Gerstner includes a 54-page appendix of memos he sent to employees. Commenting on this, Paul Sanchez, global director of employee research for Mercer Human Resource Consulting, notes that Gerstner "realized very early on that it would be impossible to move IBM without winning the hearts and minds of people."[18]

Just reading what's now in the magazines dedicated to C-suite functions is an education. Every second article appears to be about communicating. *CFO* magazine is talking about it, and *CIO* magazine advises chief information officers that "if your staff isn't doing the work you expect of them, you may be the one who needs to improve your performance."[19] You can find many other examples, but the message you should be getting is that, today, everyone in your company is part of the marketing team. Without that level of all-employee support, your company's chances of hitting a sweet spot are nil. But is one speech a year by the CEO, printed in the company newsletter, enough? Can the chief operating officer, the CIO, and the HR chief cut a video that's sent out to employees in January—and then hide the rest of the year? No way. The demand to see you, touch you, know you is enormous.

Consider this headline, based on a 427 organization, worldwide survey reported by the International Association of Business Communicators (IABC): "Only One-Third of Companies Say Their Employees Understand and Live Business Strategy in Daily Jobs." Now think about that. Translate that number to where *you* work. Are you ready to sleep tonight knowing that two out of three of your own workers haven't a clue about how your business operates, for whom, and why? It won't surprise you that, in the same article, IABC reported that "Leaders [Are] Also Not Effectively

180

Communicating with Workers at Almost Half of Employers."[20] Go ahead. Connect the dots. It is exactly as it seems: For people to trust you, they have to see you, hear you, *and* believe you.

The U.K. Department of Trade and Industry and the Chartered Management Institute teamed up to study 668 managers. The purpose of the study was to gauge the impact of organizational leaders on the work of the rest of the company. The results did not surprise me, but they may startle you: "More than half of Britain's business leaders fail to demonstrate trust, show respect for their teams, or even manage to produce results." The survey report added that managers in the United Kingdom "are crying out for business leaders who can produce what they have promised, show respect, and demonstrate trust."[21] In my experience, those results could be found in a survey of managers or workers in just about any country I've visited or worked in (and that's a lot of territory).

It's absolutely critical, then, to ask yourself these two point-blank questions; and, if the answer to either of them is *no*, proceed accordingly. Since I'm focusing on C-suite priorities, I'll take a CEO's perspective in this simple questionnaire, but any senior officer should take heed of what's suggested here:

1. *Do I spend most of my time with the public and with employees— or do I spend most of my time with my fellow C-suite allies?* If you're spending most of your time with your executive chums, it's time to seriously rearrange your working life. Stop and take stock of how poorly you're investing your time. Take control of your calendar from your secretary or assistant. Hire an executive coach. Call up a fellow CEO whom you admire. Reach out to anyone who can help you change. Do anything you have to do to change your priorities so that *most of your time in the future* is spent outside your C-suite.

2. *Can I speak for 10 minutes, without notes, on what I want my company to believe—and can I speak for an additional 10 minutes on how these beliefs translate into visible, measurable dimensions*

of our products or services? One of the legendary tales about movie pioneer Sam Goldwyn is his purported advice on becoming a great actor: *Once you can fake sincerity, you've got it made.* In a sweet spot company, there is no faking sincerity. There is simply no excuse today for a CEO who needs either cue cards or a PowerPoint presentation to capture what should be in his mind and heart. This is not to say that top executives shouldn't ever use visual aids. But if I sat across from a CEO and found that he had to refer to notes to tell me why I should want to work for his company, I would bolt (politely) out the door as soon as I could. Communications professors and consultants abound. Get one. Work one-on-one for as long as necessary, but when you emerge from your tutoring sessions, you must be able to speak from the heart. By yourself. Without notes. For 20 minutes. At least.

Until the late 90s, Patricia Wallington was corporate vice president and CIO at Xerox. Her views fit my closing message here:

Understanding how your actions affect the organization and being willing to learn new ways of leading and motivating your employees are marks of a good leader. Not only will they make you a more effective leader, but they will also help all those who look to you as a role model to be more effective. What can be better than that?[22]

Sweet Spotter: iRobot

When I hear about a company that claims, "we constantly strive to find better ways to tackle dull, dirty, and dangerous missions—with better results,"[23] I'm inclined to like it already. When I find that the company is "committed to making the world a better place by building robots that are used by people everyday,"[24] I'm intrigued. Robots? What kind of company is this?

The Whole Company Has a Dream

iRobot Corporation, the company name since 2000, has been in business since 1990 designing and developing specialized robots for clients such as the U.S. Department of Defense and the Japanese Ministry of Trade. It even designed an explorer robot for the National Geographic Society to search the Great Pyramids of Egypt.

The company founders had a dream, however: to make inexpensive, task-specific robots to do the dirty work around a home.[25] Using their own robotics knowledge and experience, and picking the brains of home cleaning experts, they conceived the Roomba, an automatic robotic vacuum. In September 2002, just prior to the holiday buying season, they introduced their invention, and home maintenance has never been the same.

They've Shown They Can Grow

Earlier that year, however, launching the product on time looked grim. Production problems kept arising, and the product wasn't finalized. Colin Angle, company cofounder and CEO, was handling the marketing himself. Since major retailers weren't interested in Roomba, Angle talked to specialty retailers like Brookstone and Sharper Image. Playing it safe, he asked the manufacturer in Hong Kong for 15,000 units, with 10,000 more possible if sales went well.

Oops! Upon receiving its first order, Brookstone wanted to buy all available Roombas, even paying for air delivery from China when a strike closed ports on the West Coast. The factory scrambled and was able to deliver 50,000 units to meet the demand. Major retailers began asking for the product; sales were over 200,000 units the first year.[26] By October 2004, Roomba sales were over 1 million units.[27]

What accounted for this surge in sales? Initial sales were to early adopters and holiday shoppers looking for unique gifts. A television ad in October 2003 introduced the Roomba to the audience beyond gadget freaks, the millions of viewers comprising the general public. In addition, the company offered new versions of the product with improved features and increased ease of use.

What's That Sound? It's Customers!

The biggest contributor to Roomba's sales, however, was customer buzz. It seemed that everyone who tried the product recommended it to a friend or bought it for a relative. Visit the company's web site today and look at the customer reviews. You couldn't ask for better recommendations. Customers don't just like Roomba; they love it!

Comments range from "My favorite appliance" to "I AM IN LOVE! Stop thinking about it and go buy one."

Customers with special needs are especially excited about it: "I have major allergies, especially to dust. . . . So, we decided to give Roomba a try. We can't believe the difference. It has truly helped my health problems." And in the same vein: "I was recently diagnosed with Multiple Sclerosis and vacuuming just took so much out of me. . . . Now, I just turn on the Roomba (I call her Rosie like so many of your customer's do, I suspect) and the place is spotless. I thank 'Rosie' everytime she goes back to her charging base. I tell everyone how great your product is. I rave about it!"[28]

They're Winning Awards

You may naturally be skeptical of enthusiastic customer reviews posted on the company web site, but many newspapers and magazines have also published rave reviews about Roomba. *Good Housekeeping* magazine even named cofounder and company chairman Helen Greiner its "Entrepreneur of the Year" in its 2006 Best Buy Awards issue.[29]

iRobot went public in late 2005 with an IPO of $24.00 per share. Since that time, it's had ups and downs, with the price as of June 25, 2006, above its public-offering price. Still, its performance is better than analysts predicted with sales increasing 123 percent over the previous year. One analyst predicts consumer sales of $134 million this year, and $164 million in 2007.[30]

They're Redefining the Marketplace

The company seems poised for future success for a number of reasons: It introduced another popular product, Scooba, a robotic floor-washing device, in 2005. It is moving into European and Asian markets, and Korea and Japan are especially interested in robots. And, finally, as our population ages, more people will be looking for products, like Roomba and Scooba, that can help them remain independent in their own homes. In fact, says CEO Angle, "[Think] about robots taking care of people, especially for elder care. That's ultimately the killer application for robotics."[31]

Employ Advocates, Not Workers

Sweet Spot Skill #5: Market from the inside out! Don't sleep easy until all employees are on the sales team. How to start? Create employee heroes. Most important, listen till it hurts.

Now might be a good time for me to ask you a question that you may have already asked yourself: What, exactly, is the primary reason why your own company is not enjoying sweet spot status? It may surprise you, but I think the answer to this thorny question might just be centered on the people working for you. How many of those fine souls—you know, the ones to whom you jovially give a wave of your hand along with a pleasant "Hello!" each morning— consider it their job to promote your brand, win over customers, and generally play in the league of sweet spot companies that now tower at the top of your industry? My guess? If you're not seeing the kind of success you think your company should have, it's probably because—when it comes to marketing your company—most of your employees are thinking, "Hey, that's not *my* job!"

A lot of comedians have made that the punch line to a joke, but when I see it crop up in almost any business context, I bristle fast. "It's not my job." The line's been around for a long time; some television personality said it over and over back in the 1950s, to great applause. Nowadays, it's sometimes said with only pseudo-humorous intent. For example, you're in a company meeting and the room turns tense as the senior manager lays out the need to cut costs or raise revenues. Ideas are proposed. Specific tasks are assigned. And someone, usually to break the tension, says "It's not my job" when an especially unpleasant task is assigned to him. Everyone laughs, including you. But was it really a joke?

Let's face it: A lot of people—without resorting to the actual words for INMJ (the acronym for "It's not my job" on the Internet)—are constantly pushing back when new duties are placed on their to-do list. You've been there. You ask someone to manage a new assignment, and the manager or employee shoots back with words and phrases like "extenuating circumstances" or "current work overload," or "an existing major backlog." This is not to say that most people in the business world today don't have more than their share of work to do. The U.S. National Institute for Occupational Safety and Health actually has a webpage devoted to the damage that can occur when anyone is over his head with work.[1]

Yet, while I concede that, in some cases, overwork is a true malady (which needs to be professionally treated), more often than not what I see are people working hard but not connecting their work to anything tangible about the business they're working for. Or, sometimes they are working very hard on things that benefit their immediate areas or just their own business units and not the entire company. Put another way, I see a lot of people working hard (including many managers) but lacking any kind of personal mission that links their labors to the success of the enterprise. They have a very siloed approach. My name for such people: they are *half-hearted* workers and managers. And I want to make it your mission to erase the population of half-hearted workers and managers inside your company by making all of them—*all of them*—part of the marketing team.

Sometimes half-heartedness comes from the kind of organization that people are working for. To my mind, there are two types of organizations: marketing-driven organizations and those that do not recognize the true role and value of marketing. Most consumer goods companies are the marketing-driven companies; while (in my experience) almost all others have trouble understanding the value of marketing. In nonmarketing-driven companies, the role of the CMO is to educate the employees starting at the top and for one salient reason: to leverage marketing to solve customer pain points.

Sadly, regardless of the type of organization, internal communication of any major marketing initiative is usually relegated to the people in human resources who seldom, if ever, know how to market. To make matters worse, the marketers do not want to challenge human resources because they believe marketers are the keepers of customer value. Thus, and again: I find this so sad, marketers too often do not have much interest in nonmarketing employees. The result: for whatever reason, the cancer of INMJ permeates most of the organization. Hence, even the best marketing concept or campaign does not work.

Half-Hearted People

Now, why should you care about half-hearted people to begin with? Let me give you a very bottom-line reason: *Half-hearted people sour the very essence of your enterprise.* Whether your business is about automobiles, hotel rooms, or trash collection, somewhere along the line someone from your company made a sale to a customer (hopefully, a lot of customers). I'm willing to bet that each sale was accompanied by four-color brochures or an eye-popping web site that dazzled the customer into thinking "Wow! *This* is great. Sign me up!" So, sale made, what do they find if, in fact, the actual delivery of your product or service hinges on half-hearted employees? They get people (representing your entire business) whose mind is focused on just about anything but happy customers.

Here's a stat you should think about for at least five minutes. Salary.com did a survey of 373 company representatives (e.g., human resources types) and 13,592 individuals. It came up with a number of findings; here was the first: "65 percent of employees plan on looking for a new job in the next three months." Here was their second finding: "Employees are more committed to their job searches than their employers anticipate." Here was their third finding: "Lower paid employees are 66 percent more likely to look for a new job than highly paid employees." And while Salary.com did report that the main reasons that employees wanted to leave their jobs were heavily driven by compensation issues, it's curious what the other top reasons were. Some 37 percent wanted to leave because they saw no room for advancement in the company; 34.2 percent felt their work was not being recognized; and 20.1 percent were plain bored.[2]

You can deny (pray?) that these statistics don't apply to your company and your employees, but I wonder just how sure you can be about that. I know, as a customer, that many times my interests seem far removed from the minds of the people who are "serving" me. It happens in grocery stores and car rental companies. Recently, I stayed at a four-star hotel that was so sluggish on room service, I not only gave up on getting a good meal—I gave up on wanting to stay with this hotel chain ever again. Sometimes I have to deal with that company again, but I would switch in *half* of a New York minute if there was a choice. For example, I subscribe to a satellite broadcast network. The leading players have millions of customers, as you know by seeing all the satellite dishes atop houses. Now, is the signal good, strong, and reliable? Yes. But I sure hate the customer service of this provider in terms of how it handles billing. Even if there is a *one dollar* difference between your bill and what your payment was, it charges *five dollars* per month delinquency fee. Seems to me that the way it has designed the billing process maximizes the chance that most people will end up paying a delinquency charge. If this satellite service didn't have the unique programming that I like, I would have been long gone. So, bad service impacts customer satisfaction and customer loyalty.

But let me be very clear about this: I don't believe that the fault for such employee-related product or service failures is completely (or even usually) tied to the people who deal face-to-face with the customer. In my experience, employees who don't give a damn are usually employees who haven't been given even one good reason to care. And that's a management problem.

So What? Who Cares?

Yet, employees who sour your workplace are also souring your customers. It's probable; no, it's inevitable. And this can happen in even the biggest companies. Wendy Kennedy writes a provocative blog about such issues; it's cleverly titled, "So what? who cares? why you?" and I took note of one of her postings that talked about the "downward spiral" that can happen when sour employees lead to sour customers:

> *When your customers aren't happy, nothing else should matter to you but getting them happy.*
>
> *Sounds trite I know but trust me when [I] say that more times than not, we don't see the warning signs of an unhappy customer (most of them don't tell us, they tell others). And so when a customer feels you're not listening or acting, they start talking with their peer group over breakfast about their problems with you. And so the downward spiral begins.[3]*

I think a lot of businesses are more inclined to be in a downward spiral than in a heated pursuit of sweet spot status. You can (and should) be measuring customer satisfaction with your company; yet, depending on the quality of the measuring devices, too many companies are deceived into thinking that it's all the other companies that are driving the negative statistics that make headlines all the time.

Rachel Fitton wrote a piece for *EuroBiz* magazine that has never really left my mind since I first read it. Talking about some research done by Ogilvy One and QCi, she asks if we realize that "only 35 percent of companies say 'thanks' to customers? That only 20 percent of companies 'have some form of formal contact strategy to welcome new customers and start to build a relationship'? That 62 percent of companies do not measure customer retention in any practical form?" But the really dangerous conclusion that Fitton reports, based on the research, is that "59 percent of companies that try to improve their customer management find 'their organization structure positively hinders the smooth transition from the creation of new customer strategies and approaches to their implementation.' To put it simply, the majority of companies will shoot themselves in the foot when they try to improve the way they deal with customers and will fail."[4]

Have I depressed you thoroughly? It's not my intent to do so. I needed to lay before you the stunning fact that a company can do a lot of things right in terms of strategic thinking and brand messaging—and still lose. It can come up with sexy new products. It can offer stellar services at the smartest of prices. *But it will all be for naught if the company's employees are not the core of your product quality and your service guarantee.* This is, in my judgment, the reason why there are so few companies that have achieved sweet spot acclaim.

Customers versus Employees

It's ironic, isn't it? Marketing experts spend most of their time thinking about how to persuade the customers and prospects to buy products and services; but only a select few recognize the important audience segment: *employees.* They are the ones who make the brand come alive for the customers and other stakeholders. I've found that so many marketers ignore this important segment (or it is done so poorly) that employees do not have any emotional attachment to what is being communicated via all the marketing channels.

Early in my own career, I became convinced that you have to make the employees your brand ambassadors. Full-circle marketing must involve everyone all of the time. Marketing really is everyone's job.

Yet, I would not want you to think that this is just a slogan. Operating so that your company allows people to do their jobs in a customer-savvy way is a great deal of work. Think now of the many different contacts one of your customers could have with your company. Sure, there's the usual sales channel (and, admittedly, that could be a human channel, a telephone channel, an Internet channel). Today, there are usually multiple customer touch points, and multichannel marketing requires a proper hand off from one functional area to another. You see, customers don't think old-school any more. Consider bookstores. In the past, a customer bought books mainly from her local store; now, she does not feel even a sliver of loyalty to any one store. The next book she might buy online. Or she might call the 800-number for Barnes & Noble.

Thus, the channels and touch points through which product and service offerings are delivered (salesforce, channel partners, Web, call centers, etc.) are dealing, more than ever, with customers expecting and demanding freedom to migrate across channels. Added to this customer-to-company complexity is the embedded organizational structure and functional responsibility within an organization. Today many call centers are managed by operations (not sales); salesforce associates report to a sales organization that is often split off from marketing. The permutations are endless. All of this puts a greater burden on efficient and effective hand offs; customers must feel welcome and responded to no matter whom they are dealing with—or when.

A not-so-funny story in this regard: AT&T Wireless, before it merged into another telecom company, spent tens of millions of dollars to launch a new service, M-life. In one night alone, the company spent more than $15 million in Super Bowl advertising to create awareness for M-life. The ads directed customers to the AT&T web site. Yes, it's *just* what you're thinking: The web site was so overloaded that consumers could not log on during and even right after the Super Bowl ads. During the following week, I decided to go to an AT&T Wireless company store to inquire about M-life. The salesperson didn't have any clue about the program (other than the Super Bowl ad). This is a total waste of $15 million—not because its employees did not care (although it sure seemed that way), but because AT&T Wireless did not bring *all* its employees into the marketing loop before launching the campaign. And it was 100 percent avoidable; all AT&T Wireless needed was a dose of managerial leadership.

Living the Brand?

That's why, when I first started at Pitney Bowes, I made sure that all marketing efforts were bidirectional, aimed *outside* the company—as well as *inside*. I was determined to make our own employees one of the most important audience segments for the ultimate success of our branding campaign. Consider this: *We did not start on external communication until we educated the employees internally.* We created an opportunity for employees to become brand ambassadors.

Inside Pitney Bowes, we created a mantra (of sorts) via our branding and internal education efforts. The goal? We wanted 35,000 employees worldwide to *think* as One Company, *act* as One Company, and *operate* as One Company—all tied together with our common brand values of being "Reliable, Trustworthy, Secure, and Innovative." This was no small goal; it was an especially daunting (and important) challenge because, when I joined Pitney Bowes, the employees had very limited knowledge of our enterprise-wide product and service offerings. As a result, we were seeing extremely limited cross selling by the salesforce.

Let's be clear about this. Our 35,000 employees are great people. They want to work for a great organization and are prepared to work day and night to make that happen. But, they can't do that if they are trapped in functional silos and can't see the big picture for all the pressure to deliver business unit success. And that was what was happening at Pitney Bowes. Through no fault of our hard working people, there was a lack of connection. The bulk of our employees could not articulate the Pitney Bowes story. And every company needs to connect with its story and to allow its people to connect.

I've mentioned some of this before. We mapped out a plan to communicate with, and seek a firm commitment from, everyone inside Pitney Bowes. First, we started working with everyone in our salesforce ranks. Reliable, Trustworthy, Secure, and Innovative: These are great words, but we went to our salesforce and asked each one "Are you, personally, living the brand?" The branding objective we set for other customer-facing employees was to persuade them to find the brand relevant (and thus, too, to live it when working with customers). Finally, the branding objective for all other employees was to clarify and make sure they were both aware of and understood the brand. (See Figure 9.1.)

FIGURE 9.1 Building Employee Commitment

As a result of all these efforts, we created a new company vision that embraced the branding that we had created and were now betting the fate of the company on. We also crafted a new set of operating principles and insisted that the first people to be trained in how to make these principles come to life were *the top 100 executives* of the company. We made sure everyone tied to our C-suite was capable of, and fully committed to, modeling our new core beliefs *before* we rolled it down to other employees. I could go on about this, but perhaps now you have a better feel for how it was that we needed to bring the top 200 leaders to a two-day meeting with the rest of the top leaders of the company going through a one-day brand education program. In addition, all sales, service, and customer-facing employees had to go through a custom built-for-them brand training program. We included how to live the brand in the yearly evaluation of every employee. And, to this day, I have no regret about carving out substantial time on my calendar to speak to more than 2,000 employees personally. You can't convert half-hearted employees and managers without being full-hearted yourself. I had to live the brand before I could ask 35,000 others to do the same.

Today, close to two-thirds of all Pitney Bowes employees and especially the salesforce can articulate what Pitney Bowes does completely and they use the brand tools to open doors with their customers. At the same time, more than half of the employees find the brand positioning relevant to their areas.

In many ways, what we did was much like the classic story of the "Quality Is Job 1" campaign of Ford Motor Company. I can cite two executives who made a big difference at Ford: Philip Caldwell and Donald Petersen. The "Job 1" campaign they started in 1979 lasted through 1997.[5] And every employee was invited (*strongly* invited) to get personally involved in the campaign to improve quality at Ford. It was a very successful program, and Petersen (who was chairman/CEO from 1980 to 1990) has had almost two decades to mull over what he now must see as his greatest career success. But, in Petersen's own words, note that the reason "Job 1" succeeded was mainly because of what *employees* did:

> *We began engaging people at all levels and in all functions in what became known as the employee involvement movement in the 1980s. Encouraging everyone to participate and channeling individual and team efforts toward well-defined common goals produced remarkable results. As measured by owner-reported "things gone wrong," vehicle quality improved more than 60 percent from 1980 to 1987 models. Breakthrough products such as the radically aerodynamic 1986 Ford Taurus helped convince consumers that American manufacturers could not only decrease defects but also increase design and engineering attributes that maximized product appeal.[6]*

It is widely known that Ford is struggling to make its current product line attractive, compelling, packed with quality, and environmentally friendly.[7] It is an enormous technological challenge, one which Petersen must love to think about. But Petersen has his focus where you need to have it; technology alone doesn't make customers want to do business with your company. Technology may represent the brand; only employees can *live* it. As Petersen says: "[Whatever] shape the technology takes and wherever it leads us, we would do well to remember the lesson we learned in the 1980s to honor and encourage the people behind new ideas."[8]

Full-Time Advocates

As I think back on what we did at Pitney Bowes, I recall a great statement that I now have to believe was part of the pizza pizzazz that has fueled the growth of Domino's Pizza. The chain now has 7,500 stores in 56 countries. Its operational motto: "If you don't make it, bake it, or take it—then you're support for those who do." You see, a company that simply employs *workers* is never going to compete with a company that employs *advocates*. That is why you need to create an internal marketing effort that is as energetic as anything you are doing out in the marketplace. Apple, FedEx, Google, Home Depot, Starbucks—this is how they started down the road of becoming sweet spot companies.

One night I caught Home Depot CEO, Bob Nardelli on *The Charlie Rose Show* talking about his philosophy of managing a company with more than 2,000 stores in the United States, Puerto Rico, Mexico, and Canada.[9] It takes some 234,000 full-time employees to operate such a massive enterprise. I was amazed at how many times Nardelli talked about the importance of communicating the company's core values, of training employees to act as "owners," and of making sure that employees don't go to work without feeling challenged, even inspired. So, how do you begin to employ advocates, not workers? Some have asserted that Nardelli's passion for unifying the Home Depot "troops" is almost akin to the military, but dig deeper and you'll see that what Nardelli and his team have done is to make Home Depot perform with an elegant formula for success. And when I say formula, I mean it:

These days everyone at Home Depot is ranked on the basis of four performance metrics: financial, operational, customer, and people skills. The company has placed human resources managers in every store, and all job applicants who make it through a first-round interview must then pass a role-playing exercise. Dennis M. Donovan, Home Depot's executive vice-president for human resources and a GE alumnus, measures the effectiveness of Home Depot workers by using an equation: VA = Q x A x E. Its meaning? According to Home Depot, the value-added (VA) of an employee equals the quality (Q) of what you do, multiplied by its acceptance (A) in the company, times how well you execute (E) the task. The goal is to replace the old, sometimes random management style with new rigor.[10]

Note, again, the importance of each and every employee. The whole performance of the company hinges on each "soldier." And whether you're fond of that analogy or not, what's key is your accepting the need to make all employees ambassadors of your brand. It starts with *communicating what's important to the people who are the most important.*

There's a gem of a book written by Ram Charan that I want you to read. The title? *What the CEO Wants You to Know.*[11] In his preface to the book, Ram makes an essential point about mastering the corporate world:

When you come right down to it, business is very simple. There are universal laws of business that apply whether you sell fruit from a stand or are running a Fortune 500 company. . . . The best CEOs and the man or woman running the one-person shop think the same way. They know their cash situation. They know what items are profitable and which are not. They understand the importance of keeping their products moving off the shelf—inventory velocity— and they know their customers.[12]

What Ram is getting at is an increasingly relevant term for you: *business acumen.*

I have felt, for years, that a lot of what passes as internal communications inside most companies is information that is one level higher than "Hello! How are you?" It's normal, in lots of companies, to see top officers (when they take the time) talking about how the company is doing in the broadest of terms. Rarely do I see companies talking openly, fully, and earnestly to employees up and down the organizational chart about the rudiments of the business—especially about the strategies and tactics that will make their brand a successful one in the marketplace.

Focus your efforts on business education—and not just any business, your business. Employees get a lot of communication, especially in a global company. My advice is to link your communication to what's affecting your customers and how your company is responding. Build a dialog with your employees. This means that the basics of business—again, what Ram Charan calls *business acumen*—must be the language of your presentations. And, as with any language, you must be sure that everyone inside your company receives enough training to both understand and speak the language of business. There's a cost to such an education and communications campaign, but the payoff is real, too: It's the elimination of a half-hearted workforce. I'm betting that greater profits will soon follow.

Bring the Brand Alive for the Employees

One of the inexplicable norms in the business world is this conundrum. Why is it that CEOs will unthinkingly sign off on an external marketing campaign that costs millions of dollars yet choke when it comes to spending thousands of dollars on employee involvement? I see this so often that I think many corporate leaders no longer think about it. But you don't help employees live the corporate brand by boring them. You have to make the brand come alive for the employees the same way you would for customers or external shareholders.

Thus, all the questions you would ask *before* you go out to a major customer with a new presentation should be asked before you meet with a group of your own employees:

What are we trying to tell them? How do we snag their interest? How do we keep their interest? How do we make sure the presentation is compelling? How do we keep it short enough to keep the pace lively while making sure we include enough detail? What materials should they have during the presentation? What materials should they have at the conclusion of the presentation? What do we expect from the audience, in terms of follow-up action? How can we test whether our message got through? How can we test how much they remember in 30 days? In 90 days? In 180 days? How can we motivate them not only to believe what we say but also to transmit this information to others?

In other words, you have to win the hearts of your employees the same way you plan, and plan, and then plan some more to win the hearts and minds of your best (and future) customers. It is *that* important. And, lest anyone be misled that what I'm proposing here is cheerleading, think again: You need to act on every word that you utter in regard to getting your employees to start thinking with customers and your brand in mind. All of this is not meant to be a "Rah! Rah!" exercise. The core purpose of what I'm proposing here are employee ranks that enjoy both more meaningful engagement with the top tiers of the company *and*, as a result, more meaningful work by seeing how their efforts yield stronger customer ties.

Ever hear of Sir John Harvey-Jones? Quite possibly you have not. He was a star in British business back in the 1980s; in fact, he rose from being a minor player in the work study department of Imperial Chemical Industries (ICI) to become chairman of the international conglomerate in 1982. He then went on to become the author of numerous business books and even starred in a business-related television show.[13] In his own way, Sir John was thinking about the whole idea of what it takes to make a sweet spot company back in 1988 when he wrote *Making It Happen*. I have read, and reread, the third chapter of that book many times. It's all about "switching on or switching off" a company. In the first mode, the organization is throbbing as one body to make the business successful;

in the second mode, it's a lethargic company populated by half-hearted worker bees. As he points out, deciding where you want to take your company is only the start of your work. You have to determine how you can "switch on" the rest of your workforce. You have to realize that the top of the company is, in this sense, the least-important part of the company:

> *Supposing we have decided, broadly, where we want to go, the problem then becomes how to get there, how to make it happen. This is of course where many good business ideas fail. Part of the secret . . . is the way in which we discuss again and again our ideas and proposals up and down the company, continuously adjusting, altering and probing our positions until, at last, we reach a conclusion which we can all accept and work to. In deciding where we should go we have to transfer "ownership" of the direction by involving everyone in the decision. Making it happen means involving the hearts and minds of those who have to execute and deliver.* It cannot be said often enough that these are not the people at the top of the organization, but those at the bottom. [emphasis mine]

I have always advocated that the amount of energy spent on educating workers and managers about marketing issues should be directly proportional to the amount of time each employee spends affecting the satisfaction of a customer. Obviously, then, you'd spend more time (and effort) with sales personnel than you would with the janitorial staff. But please note that it is *also* important to include everyone in the company quest to achieve sweet spot status. You can't afford to leave anyone in the dark; for that entry-level employee might just know someone who knows someone who knows a key contact inside your largest customer. Get the picture? Then, starting now, strive to get everyone on board.

Let Your Employees Do Heroic Things

I heard a fantastic story about a FedEx employee who put the cost of hiring a helicopter on his personal American Express card so he could help FedEx keep its business operating during a blizzard. "Very impressive," I can hear you say, "but very unusual." Okay, I agree. But I think you are really discounting the story too much if you do not realize that there are many businesses that celebrate the heroic acts of its employees. And you don't have to be in the high-charm world of "absolutely positively overnight" FedEx to do so.

Waste Management (WM) is in the trash collection business. Now, enterprise does not get more dull and boring than that, right? You can't make heroes out of guys who drive a garbage truck, right? There are no moments of truth in the business of trash, right? Wrong. Wrong. Wrong. Here's how Waste Management sees it, as a company:

> *Waste Management's 50,000+ employees are dedicated to serving the communities in which they live and work. They share your concerns about safety, the environment and the well-being of their neighbors. Because they are on the streets every day, our employees get a first-hand view of how their job performance and attention to detail impacts the lives of so many others.*
>
> *At Waste Management, we take pride in the good works our employees perform every day. We're happy to have this opportunity to share some true stories about our employees that highlight their outstanding citizenship, their selfless acts of heroism and their dedication to service in the community.[14]*

Waste Management spotlights those employees who did more than collect trash on the day when a woman was drowning, when a toddler crawled in front of a stopped trash truck's front tire, when seven people were trapped inside a burning car, and when 30 high school students were unwittingly working inside a burning building.[15]

But heroism does not have to be life and death in nature. There are the heroics of an employee who helps a customer meet a critical deadline, of a service tech who stays with a distress phone call after the posted end-of-day hour has come and gone, or of an engineer who spots a major problem with a new product in design and stops it before the product goes into full-scale production. The question is not the degree of heroism but whether you and your company take time to spot, recognize, announce, and elevate heroic behavior so that everyone in the company sees that living the brand also means going the extra mile, when it's called for, to transform citizens into potential customers and existing customers into raving fans.

So, right now, if you can't name 10 heroes inside your own company—people that others inside the organization would list as heroes as well—then perhaps it's time to set some new priorities where you work.

Listen for the Sound of Marketing Coming Alive

I know that many of you who are not marketing professionals think that marketers practice communications in only one mode and that mode is telling the world about the products and services that they are paid to promote. But, know what, the best marketers I've ever known have been, first, good listeners. That's precisely how they learn so much from their encounters with customers and prospects. And, guess what: The same principle applies to bringing everyone else in the company onto the marketing team.

Lyman Steil and Richard Bommelje, in my opinion, wrote *the* book on listening, *Listening Leaders*. In it, these two pioneers in the field of effective listening catalog how listening can be converted to concrete knowledge that can help a company react and respond to marketplace trends. Early in the book, Bill Kroll, a district sales manager with Colgate Oral Pharmaceuticals, defines listening "as the act of acknowledging the unique value of the thoughts and opinions of others."[16] But the comment that overlapped completely with my own view of the world was the comment by Peter Nulty, who made it to *Fortune*'s National Business Hall of Fame. Read this comment aloud—and listen:

Of all the skills of leadership, listening is the most valuable, and one of the least understood. Most captains of industry listen only sometimes, and they remain ordinary leaders. But a few, the great ones, never stop listening.[17]

I can't pretend, here, to try to teach you fully how to improve a skill that is absolutely critical in any sweet spot company. Effective listening requires that you: (1) hear fully what someone else is saying, (2) capture (and if you can, commit to memory) the content of what you heard, (3) acknowledge to the speaker that you have heard by summarizing what he or she has said, and (4) most important, act on what you heard in a way that reflects the normal expectations of the person(s) you are listening to.

What I can say is that Peter Nulty's point is spot-on. Consider Nucor Steel, the upstart steelmaker that at one time was a small-time competitor to the big guys, like U.S. Steel, and is now a sweet spot business with $12.7 billion in sales. In its early days, Ken Iverson was the company chief who had a radical view of how to manage: "that employees, even hourly clock-punchers, will make an extraordinary effort if you reward them richly, treat them with respect, and give them real power." According to Iverson the single most important skill of any leader is to "listen, listen, listen." *BusinessWeek* reported on Nucor:[18]

At Nucor the art of motivation is about an unblinking focus on the people on the front line of the business. It's about talking to them, listening to them, taking a risk on their ideas, and accepting the occasional failure. It's a culture built in part with symbolic gestures. Every year, for example, every single employee's name goes on the cover of the annual report. . . .

At times, workers and managers exhibit a level of passion for the company that can border on the bizarre. Executive Vice-President Joseph A. Rutkowski, an engineer who came up through the mills, speaks of Nucor as a "magic" place, representing the best of American rebelliousness. He says "we epitomize how people should think, should be." [Executive Vice-President John J. Fer-riola] goes even further: "I consider myself an apostle" for the gospel of Ken Iverson. "After Christ died, people still spread the word. Our culture is a living thing. It will not die because we will not let it die, ever."

Whether you like the example set by Ken Iverson and Nucor or not, the point to take home to your own company today is simply this: By listening to your employees (as hard, or harder, than you listen to your customers), you can learn a great deal about what *they* see as the key trends in the marketplace and the major concerns of customers. Sometimes, such listening can be downright painful. But if you listen till it hurts, you will be amazed at how it will improve your leadership. Or, as Steil and Bommelje put it: "Believing that the quality and character of a leader determines the performance and results, the success of our leadership depends on how effectively we mobilize our people around our mission and values and vision, and how effectively all of our people listen to the customer."[19]

Sweet Spotter: Texas Roadhouse

In the competitive world of moderately priced restaurants, what makes Texas Roadhouse stand out? Crystal Petrocelli, a restaurant reviewer in Arizona, captures the way many of this restaurant chain's fans see it:

> *Service:* So shockingly accommodating it's like the manager just walked out of a Customers Rule! Seminar.
>
> The young hostess grabs a basket of golden rolls for us, asks how we're doing and gives us the scoop on Texas Roadhouse. Our server swoops in as

the hostess leaves. Drink orders are taken and our beverages are brought out a minute or two later. . . .

Meal: You can't eat just one of the soft rolls smeared with cinnamon apple whipped butter.

The 18-ounce T-Bone and 16-ounce New York Strip live up to their listed sizes and look lovely with diamond-shaped grill marks. They're juicy and cooked medium as requested. They're not as tender or flavorful as, say, the $40-and-up steaks at fancier places, but they're good and you can't beat the price. . . .

Scene: The first things you notice are sizzling steaks on the grill and peanut shells on the floor.

It's a little loud thanks to a country-loving jukebox and packed house. The chaos seems to fade away once we're in our booth. . . .

If work weren't buying: This is the rare occasion where waiting 30 minutes on a Monday night to eat a franchise fillet is not totally insane. They don't take reservations, but if you call two hours ahead of time you'll be put on a list that helps you score a table faster.[20]

Another customer, not a professional reviewer, and his family waited 45 minutes for a table on a Friday night. "It's way better," said the customer. "The atmosphere's better. The food's better. It's not so old-fashioned. It has a younger atmosphere. Waiting in line is not a big deal because you're having a better meal."[21] So what's the Texas Roadhouse secret to success?

Know What You Offer and What You Stand For

Better atmosphere, better food, better service: It all sounds like a formula for standing out from the crowd.

"We are value players in the casual space," says company chief executive Gerard Hart. "We are the Southwest Airlines of the casual-dining space. We do it really well, and we are going to continue to do what we do." Company founder Kent Taylor puts it this way, "We wanted to provide a place that the whole family could enjoy. Texas Roadhouse is about a hearty, good meal with service that is friendly, energetic, and enthusiastic."[22]

They Understand the Segment They're Serving

Founded in 1993 in (ironically) Indiana, Texas Roadhouse has grown to over 225 restaurants in 42 states. The company focuses mainly on mid-sized suburban and rural markets, with over 30 percent of its restaurants located in the Midwest. The restaurants serve only dinner during the week, with lunch offered on Saturday and Sunday. This strategy keeps down not only labor costs, but also real estate costs, because the company can site its restaurants away from downtown areas serving business lunches: CEO Hart likens it to a Wal-Mart strategy. Taylor, the founder, still personally selects all sites for future restaurants; however, when it comes to pleasing you or the millions of other diners who frequent Texas Roadhouse, there are some 15,000 employees attending to every customer's whim.

They Make Their Customers Their Best Advertisement

The company advertises very little, instead spending money on training its managers so that word-of-mouth comments are positive; in fact, the company motto is "Legendary Food, Legendary Service." Indeed, the company was voted #1 steakhouse in a consumer survey in 2003. The company web site offers customers' testimonials to the superb service they have received. A high server-to-customer ratio means that customers get more attention here than in other restaurants; this, in turn, promotes one of the industry's fastest ratios of table turnover.[23]

They Thrive on Adversity

The company has suffered setbacks common to many in the industry: Hurricane Katrina hit Gulf Coast businesses hard and high energy costs affected results. But the company locked in prices on beef, which accounts for 46 percent of its food budget; saved a little on pork; and reduced costs on chicken by 10 percent. In addition, average annual sales per restaurant are $3.7 million, among the highest in the industry.

Texas Roadhouse shares have increased in value about 80 percent since the company went public in October 2004, and the company is growing about 25 percent per year. Despite competition from chains such as Outback Steakhouse, Logan's Roadhouse, and Lone Star Steakhouse, analysts are positive about the company's future. Malcolm Knapp dismissed threats from the competition: "Steak is American ethnic. It's basic to the American psyche. The market still has room."[24]

CHAPTER
10

The Stuff That Marketing Is Made Of

If you come to a fork in the road, take it.[1]

—Yogi Berra, Baseball Wit

Jim Hahn is the owner and president of a printing business in Louisville, Kentucky. He's built his enterprise by creating a solid brand in a highly competitive industry. Jim's store, Omni Graphics Printing & Copying, offers high quality, low prices, and the fastest turnaround on orders, bar none, in his marketplace. But I mention Jim because of a thought he shared recently. You see, Jim is a sports nut who loves to attend live sports of all kinds. Is he dedicated? You might say that; Jim has attended games in almost every major league ballpark. But, perhaps more telling, you know all those baseball cards you had as a kid and then somehow lost or misplaced as you became a corporate globetrotter? *Well, Jim never lost his cache of cards.* He still has hundreds of them. And, among his prized collection, you can find numerous baseball legends, like Tom Seaver, Dave Winfield, and Nolan Ryan. Yet, it was not his collection that brings Jim to mind right now. It's something he says about the *attitude* of a master baseball card collector: "In this hobby," Jim shares, "there's only one goal. You think of a superstar and try to find the card of that player when he was a rookie."

Sweet Rookies

In many ways, that's exactly what this book has been all about. If you had been able to predict with a high degree of certainty that:

- Apple was destined to become the magnificent company that it is,
- FedEx was to become the gold standard of delivery services,

- Starbucks was going to reinvent the traditional coffee house and make itself into a global brand,
- Home Depot was to grow into a global provider of repair and construction materials and equipment, and
- Pitney Bowes was going to grow out of being "just a postage meter company" to define and lead an entirely new category, Mailstream.

You would probably be a very happy investor! The first point to remember is this: Every sweet spot company was once a "rookie" in which someone invested their funds (or their career). I don't believe for a minute that the destiny of these companies (or any of those I've named as sweet spotters) was *just* luck. Go back through all the corporate histories of sweet spot companies (much as I have) and you will see a strong, deliberate, consistent pattern. That pattern is so strong that it's undeniable in terms of how it influenced the outcome of their strategic thinking and stellar success.

Apple knew it was *moving the marketplace* with every techno breakthrough it pioneered. We at Pitney Bowes knew we would *become much more of an alluring investment* if we embraced our postage meter traditions *and* became a company with much stronger ways to help customers manage their communications flow. Look at the early days of Google; look at its first web search tools; look at its initial capabilities and product offerings. Day by month by year, Google got better—*outdating its own innovations* with new and better ways of doing Web searches—and it knew exactly what it was doing when making its past success just that, something that happened in the past.

Starbucks, as it added ever-yummier coffee drinks to its menu (and music, and plush seating, and delicious sandwiches and cakes), knew that people would notice this and tell others. In short, the company set out *to create a boffo buzz* and measured its success not just by revenue streams and profit margins but by how many customers were talking passionately—raving—about their Starbucks experience.

213

Last, as courtly and circumspect as Fred Smith is as the founder and driver of FedEx, the energy that you see in the company today came from his *Spark Z-Leadership*. It happened because Smith knew that passion in the CEO's office alone would never be enough to energize the 216,000 employees he probably hoped would catch his fever to deliver things "absolutely, positively overnight." And so Smith and his top team cloned not only their operating savvy but also their attitude and swagger. It's the only way to explain the fierce dedication you experience any time you come face-to-face with a FedEx employee—anywhere on the planet.

Sweet Parents

However, rookies don't grow into sweet spotters without a set of skills that make them capable of becoming world-class. Golfing great Greg Norman is attributed with this touching, if Yogi Berra-like, thought: "I owe a lot to my parents, especially my mother and father."[2] Know what, that's also one way to look at sweet spot companies. They grow into the major players that they are because they have *two* great influences to shape their destiny. First, they rigidly and earnestly adhere to the six performance standards I just described. Second, they have committed themselves to make those standards doable. It's not enough to yearn to compete in the Olympics; you have to train assiduously to be able to compete. That's why I dedicated whole chapters to the critical importance sweet spot companies place on:

- *Mining minds:* They learn to march to the beat of the buyer, their customer base—the only people who can make it possible for a company to grow. They really try to understand what drives their customers and then transform that marketing knowledge into operational drivers for the company.
- *Demarcating demand:* They shun the temptation to be like everyone else and instead seek to re-invent the market-

214

place by doing everything the customer expects now—*and add yet more features that the customer will admire in the future.*

- *From logo to icon:* They know that, in business, imitation is the surest path to competitive suicide. Thus, they make their brand into something that is not just a flag to help identify the company in the marketplace. In essence, they make their brand into a bond—a promise, a pledge—that guarantees the customer an experience that is both mind pleasing and wallet smart no matter how many transactions the customer has with the company.

- *Creating champions-in-chief:* They know that the people at the top of any company must be more than watchdogs and sign-off specialists. CEO, COO, CFO, CIO: In sweet spot companies these are not the "organizational island" leaders that you find in most lackluster enterprises. What unites these C-suite officers is one special charge that sweet spot companies demand of their top execs: *become part of the marketing organization and thus go forth and campaign for our company, its product, and its brand.*

- *Employing advocates, not workers:* They know that a few officers at the top of the company are not enough—not anywhere near enough—to create an organization that dazzles both Wall Street and Main Street alike. To do this, everyone inside the company must know that, on any given day, *anyone* (no matter where he or she resides on the hierarchy) can become a hero by bringing the brand to life in such a vivid way that customers want to exalt the fact that they have chosen *this* company to buy from.

Greg Norman may owe a lot to his parents; sweet spot companies owe a lot to their chosen standards of performance and their boundless dedication to becoming every bit as good as they know they can be. Indeed, they dedicate themselves to being every bit as good as their customers hope they will become.

Champions in Crisis

Can Roger Federer lose at Wimbledon? Can Brazil lose at the World Cup? Can the Dallas Mavericks lose the NBA Finals? Can the New York Yankees strike out of the World Series? In all cases, yes. Champions are born to be tested. The question is whether a loss becomes a permanent setback. Every great enterprise must ask itself if its success signals sweet spot status or if its success is merely a historical blip.

To be sure, I don't want you to think that *all one has to do* is set standards and sharpen skills and—voila!—one becomes (or stays) a sweet spot company. Every company is at peril in an extremely dynamic marketplace. At one point, Fred Smith almost had to abandon FedEx to make his family (and other shareholders) happy. Apple actually fired Steve Jobs when his vision of the company did not seem to have sufficient traction to compete against the likes of every Windows-based computer maker. Starbucks has been hit more than once by protesters who certainly made enjoying a cup of joe a difficult thing on that particular day. But, in each case—no, *in every case*, sweet spot companies find ways to overcome the crisis of the hour and to regain their balance via their standards and their skills.

Let me add some personal testimony to this. Every brand and every company goes through a crisis at some point. Think of Merck and Vioxx, Johnson & Johnson with Tylenol, and so on. At these not-so-sweet points, all the things I have talked about come into their own. If you understand your company's sweet spot DNA, have a strong brand, are closely in touch with consumers, and have great champions-in-chief you can turn adversity into triumph. At these points, any weakness will be highlighted.

For Pitney Bowes, our crisis point came just as the world was still reeling from the tragedies of 9/11. The crisis was a bioterrorist threat to the mail, the anthrax scare that made people everywhere feel unsafe and suspicious about opening the mail. Commerce was threatened. Business and consumer mail dropped. Advertisers reduced their reliance on the mail. The U.S. Con-

216

gress shut down offices to check out potential threats. Pundits declared that mail was dead. For Pitney Bowes, the leading provider of mail and document management solutions to companies all over the world, and for our two million customers, it was a defining moment.

What We Did, What We Learned

No one enjoys being in a genuine crisis. Too many really bad things can happen; and they can happen to more than just your bottom line for the company. When a crisis hits, both corporate and personal reputations are on the line. In looking back at the anthrax threat we successfully overcame, I can think of several lessons that I learned then and recall quite clearly today:

Lesson 1: Prepare for everything and take responsibility. We had contingency plans for dealing with emergencies. Unfortunately, no one could have anticipated this particular crisis. Nevertheless, as the industry leader, we felt we had a heightened responsibility to mount a response that would not only protect our own business, but also help our customers and the general public. This was especially challenging, given the scientific uncertainty surrounding bio-terrorism and the fast-growing fear that it triggered.

Lesson 2: Act. Having taken responsibility, you need to act. First, we set up a crisis management team drawn from every function and business unit to get as broad a range of input as possible. Our immediate concern was for the safety and well-being of our frontline employees in outsourced corporate mail centers. We provided them with additional protocols for safe mail handling, methods for detection of suspicious mail, and emergency procedures. Next, we set up an emergency multichannel communication network that constantly funneled information updates to employees. Our CEO broadcast weekly voice-mail messages, and we posted these talks on our company Intranet web site and distributed the information via broadcast e-mail. Along the way we worked closely with the U.S. Postal Service and the FBI to keep abreast of the latest developments with respect to incidents and their investigations.

Lesson 3: Communicate constantly. When the going gets tough, a communication vacuum is the very last thing you need. Sharing knowledge and resources is essential. We developed an advertising campaign. The tone and manner of the campaign was direct, factual, and reassuring. We created and launched a specialized web site with critical mail security information and links to additional resources. We quickly scanned all of our mail safety resources and organized this information in a booklet mailed to 15,000 senior executives of Fortune 1000 companies. Our CEO, Mike Critelli, became the *de facto* spokesperson for the industry.

Lesson 4: Don't forget what you learned. Looking at the experience from a marketing point of view, we took an unfortunate, unanticipated situation and chose to focus on the needs of our customers and the external community, while maintaining a respectful attitude and professional stance. The result was remarkable for us as well as for our customers and the public. The role we played and the information we offered during the crisis resulted in a more positive perception of our brand and capability. We achieved greater awareness of our products and services with users as well as decision makers at higher levels of enterprise organizations. Our relationships with our customers were greatly enhanced by the perceived value we contributed during the crisis.

For us as a company, the anthrax crisis brought us together. Speaking to the world as one company was a radical departure from the past. Because everyone worked as a team, we created and launched our advertising and media campaigns and mail security web site in record time, building company confidence.

The crisis made the organization far more receptive to the ongoing coordination of other (noncrisis) marketing initiatives and to creating a marketing vision for the enterprise. It also gave me a chance to evaluate our current marketing practices and to build a plan to develop a coordinated marketing effort for the enterprise for all our products and services.

Marketing Makes the Difference

Yet it's not just a crisis that enables one to say that marketing made the difference between a corporate disaster and sweet spot resilience. My belief, and I've emphasized this throughout the book, is that marketing makes the difference in all sweet spot companies. For more than a year, I have been standing in front of audiences around the world testifying to the fact that a company headed for, or now enjoying, sweet spot status has: (1) special standards, (2) unique skills, and (3) modern marketing. Did you catch that modifier before the word "marketing"? I do believe we have come to a fork in the road for most companies. The delineation between traditional marketing and modern marketing could not be clearer. And it will be impossible for any company to achieve sweet spot acclaim if it clings to an old-school view of what its marketing organization should be and do.

This divide between traditional and modern marketing starts and ends in the minds of the people leading your company. If your leadership team looks at customers as sheep who need to be herded into buying anything you put before them, you're living in the past. If your leadership team thinks that customers can be tricked into buying your company's products and services because—hey, what do *they* know?—then you're driving your company into a permanent state of crisis. If your leadership team thinks that marketing is 100 percent emotional, that customers buy when they have been titillated into a state of buy-anything frenzy, then your company is headed for a most painful sour spot.

You see: All the old, hoary truths of Marketing 101 (or Marketing 901) classes in the year 1907 won't wash, won't hold, won't work in 2007. Today's professional marketers aren't wizards who yell and scream until the marketplace notices them. Moreover, they sure aren't people who, in essence, ferret out customers who don't want—but can be *forced* to buy—a product or service line. That's just not the way it works any more. Meryl K. Evans and Hank Stroll wrote an article titled "Marketing Challenge: Traditional vs. New Marketing." Their opening words should be read aloud in the next meeting of your corporate leadership team:

> *In today's marketplace, customers have more power than ever before. Marketing must change how it works if it is to better meet customer demands. Two things that the market has forced marketing to change are focus and control.*
>
> *[Traditional] marketing methods are beginning to be replaced by new marketing approaches—changing from being company-focused to being more consumer-focused. And the message is no longer controlled by sales, marketing, or even the CEO; it's now controlled by customers.*[3]

Connections That Count

Modern marketing, then, is all about *connecting* with customers in as many ways as your company can. Modern marketing is as much about educating as it is about selling. Modern marketing respects (and therefore offers a healthy balance between) the forces of emotional appeal and logical thinking; customers are not computers, but they do have more knowledge than ever before and need to be recognized for their minds as well as their hearts. Modern marketing values a long-term relationship with a customer over a short-term spike in sales. It's just not enough to close a deal and "move on," as old marketers used to say. And that's why modern marketing is as much about the future as it is about the present. Put another way, it's important for modern marketers to connect with customers, now, in the ways that they want to be communicated with. However, the real value of marketing in the twenty-first century is that it should help everyone inside the company to travel into the future *with* the customer. In fact, modern marketers are just as eager to find out what their customers will want next year as they are to fulfill a customer's purchase order today.

I shared with you, at the very start of this book, that "I am a marketer at heart." That used to be a statement that would place one in a corporate silo. Not any more. Marketing is the suture that connects every part of the organizational body into one robust, muscular, poised, confident, determined, capable company. But this promotion of marketing is by no means intended to be a demotion of any other function, division, or area of any company. I guess I'm strongly echoing something that Professor Philip Kotler said. Kotler, of the Kellogg School of Management at Northwestern University, is the author of numerous books on marketing; each of his books is solid reading and best-selling. You could say that he wrote (or, at least, co-authored) *the* textbook on modern marketing. But Professor Kotler is traveling the world with a strong message about how marketing needs to change. He made many interesting points when he presented "Making Marketing Work in the New Century" to an audience in Kiev, Ukraine; but one of the eight conclusions in his talk is that "marketing must become the driver of business strategy."[4]

To my mind, marketing must become the driver—the spark plug—of the modern corporation. No one else can do it because no one else is, by common assent, the link between the company and its customers. If you watched the basketball feats of the Miami Heat as they won the NBA Finals in 2006, you know that the Most Valuable Player of the series was Miami's Dwayne Wade. If there ever was a spark plug for what surely is the start of, quite probably, a sweet spot surge for Miami that will last many years, it was Dwayne Wade. Yet, as *Time*'s Sean Gregory reported, here was a player who was, years before, the most improbable rookie destined to become a champion:

> *He certainly deserves most of the compliments—he did average 34 points a game in the finals, in one of the most dominating individual performances in recent NBA history. And indeed, Wade's aerial*

escapades may eventually catch up to [the legendary Michael] Jordan's. But for the moment, let Michael just be the greatest player of all time. And let Wade be the best player in the world right now.

[But] no one predicted Wade's stunning ascension to the top of the basketball world. He wasn't one of the overhyped high school stars who expect everything handed to them. While growing up in a suburb near Chicago's South Side, idolizing [Michael] Jordan's Bulls, Wade was seriously recruited by only three colleges. He chose Marquette, in Milwaukee. "My hope was just that he would get some quality playing time at Marquette," says Wade's high school coach, Jack Fitzgerald. But he has improved his game every year in college and the pros. . . .[5]

You or your company may be sitting now, as Dwayne Wade was a few years back, with nothing but the highest of professional standards and the firmest of personal commitments to building the skills necessary to soar to the top of your chosen league. Now, if you redefine and apply the many ways that modern marketing can help transform your quest into a new reality for your company, there really is nothing that can stop you for very long. *Create your own opportunity*, and don't let anyone limit the power and sweep of your vision. *Leverage your marketing*, as it is the singular force that can tag your opportunity with a brand of product quality and customer service that will not go out of date nor out of style. *Maximize your business* in ways that are both financially sweet but, perhaps more important, historically sweet.

Vince Lombardi, the legendary coach who led the Green Bay Packers in their longest stretch of sweet spot victories, believed that "life's battles don't always go to the stronger or faster man. But sooner or later the man who wins, is the man who thinks he can."[6] It you want your company to become an Apple, a Starbucks, a FedEx, or a Pitney Bowes, I can testify that so much of that achievement starts with how you and your fellow leaders think about the challenge. In the years ahead, a lot of "corporate rookies" will emerge as marketplace titans. They're thinking about that achievement right now.

Are you?

Notes

Introduction

1. Cited in *The Week* (June 23, 2006).
2. Cited in *Newsweek* (June 26, 2006).

Chapter 1

1. http://en.thinkexist.com/quotes/michael_jordan.
2. Sergio Zyman, *The End of Marketing as We Know It* (New York: HarperCollins, 2000).
3. "An Interview with Sergio Zyman," http://www.zibs.com/zyman .shtml.
4. Gail McGovern and John Quelch, "The Fall and Rise of the CMO," *Strategy and Business*, No. 37 (Winter 2004), pp. 44-51.
5. http://www.wm.edu/news/?id=2797.
6. http://goingglobal.corante.com/archives/2006/02/22/walmart_15 _countries_and_counting.php.
7. http://www.thomaslfriedman.com/worldisflat.htm.
8. Chuck Lucier, Paul Kocourek, and Rolf Habbel, "The Crest of the Wave," *Strategy and Business*, No. 43 (Summer 2006).

Chapter 2

1. http://www.rogerfederer.com/en/fanzone/askroger/index .cfm?uNC=78575340&uPage=5.
2. http://www.bp.com/productsservices.do?categoryId=37 &contentId=2007985.

3. http://mediastockblog.com/article/6005.
4. Roben Farzad and Ben Elgin, "Googling for Gold," *BusinessWeek* (December 5, 2005).
5. http://news.yahoo.com/s/nm/20060326/bs_nm/swiss_ikea_kamprad_dc.
6. http://news.com.com/Lenovos+next+chief+looks+to+the+future/2008–1003_3–5485658.html.
7. http://www.csmonitor.com/2005/0630/p13s02-stct.html.
8. http://www.iht.com/articles/2006/04/10/business/lenovo.php
9. See note 8.
10. See note 8.
11. http://www.enron.com/corp/pressroom/releases/2001/ene/15-MostInnovative-02–06-01-LTR.html.
12. http://www.businessweek.com/1997/28/b353529.htm.

Chapter 3

1. www.famous-quotes-and-quotations.com/sports-quote.html.
2. *Renovate to Innovate: Building Performance-Driven Marketing Organizations* (CMO Council, November, 2005).
3. http://strategis.ic.gc.ca/epic/internet/instco-levc.nsf/en/h_qw00016e.html.
4. Richard H. Cox, *Sport Psychology: Concepts and Applications* (New York: McGraw-Hill, 2006).
5. http://www.humankinetics.com/products/showexcerpt.cfm?excerpt_id=3630.
6. Shane Murphy, *The Sport Psych Handbook* (Champaign, IL: Human Kinetics, 2005).
7. "This Apple Is Too Shiny," *Forbes* (January 30, 2006).
8. http://news.bbc.co.uk/1/hi/in_depth/uk/2000/newsmakers/1768724.stm.
9. http://www.businessweek.com/bwdaily/dnflash/oct2004/nf20041012_4018_db083.htm.
10. http://www.creatingcustomerevangelists.com/resources/evangelists/steve_jobs.asp.
11. http://www.usnews.com/usnews/biztech/articles/051205/5eeevangelist.htm.
12. http://www.businessweek.com/magazine/content/06_06/b3970001.htm.

13. "Why FedEx Is Flying High," *Fortune* (November 1, 2004).
14. http://money.cnn.com/2006/03/17/magazines/fortune/csuite_fedex _fortune_040306/index.htm.
15. http://www.google.com/corporate/index.html.
16. http://www.hamline.edu/administration/libraries/search/comparisons .html.
17. http://p6.hostingprod.com/@www.ventureblog.com/articles/indiv /2003/000080.html.
18. http://biz.yahoo.com/ap/060505/microsoft_ballmer.html?.v=3.
19. http://www.businessweek.com/magazine/content/05_49/b3962001 .htm.
20. "Pitney Bowes Describes Growth Opportunities in Global Mail-stream Market," http://money.cnn.com/services/tickerheadlines /prn/200603030900PR_NEWS_USPR____NYF031.htm.
21. http://www.techworld.com/mobility/features/index.cfm?featureid =708&Page=3&pagePos=3.
22. http://www.koffeekorner.com/koffeehistory.htm.
23. http://www.starbucks.com/aboutus/overview.asp.
24. http://www.businessweek.com/bw50/2006/24.htm.
25. Howard Schultz, *Pour Your Heart into It: How Starbucks Built a Company One Cup at a Time* (New York: Hyperion, 1999).

Chapter 4

1. www.baseball-almanac.com.
2. http://www.bbc.co.uk/wales/raiseyourgame/dedication/best_you _can/renaldo_nehemiah.shtml.
3. http://en.wikipedia.org/wiki/Jeff_Gordon.
4. http://sportsillustrated.cnn.com/features/1997/nascar/nshend.html.
5. Cited in *Newsweek* (June 26, 2006).
6. Edward Landry, Andrew Tipping, and Jay Kumar, "Growth Champions," *Strategy and Business* (Summer 2006).
7. http://www.blueoceanstrategy.com.
8. Stuart Crainer and Des Dearlove, "New Partners in Healthcare," *Think: Act*, vol. 3, no. 1 (March 2006).
9. http://en.thinkexist.com/quotation/i_think_self-awareness_is _probably_the_most/199694.html.
10. *Renovate to Innovate: Building Performance-Driven Marketing Organizations* (CMO Council, November 2005).

Chapter 5

1. http://crmguru.infopop.cc/groupee/forums/a/tpc/f/6426008265/m/4046008265.
2. http://www.businessweek.com/bwdaily/dnflash/oct2004/nf20041012_4018_db083.htm.
3. http://www.crm2day.com/news/crm/EplVVyEkuEWYtnYpmD.php.
4. http://www.keynote.com/news_events/releases_2006/06jan19.html.
5. Daniel Yankelovich and David Meer, "Rediscovering Market Segmentation," *Harvard Business Review* (February 2006).
6. http://www.bizlogx.com/ccselling.pdf.
7. Richard Whiteley, *The Customer-Driven Company* (Reading, MA: Perseus Books, 1993).
8. http://us.penguingroup.com/nf/Book/BookDisplay/0,,9781591841098,00.html.
9. http://www.jetblue.com/learnmore/index.html.
10. http://blog.washingtonpost.com/thecheckout/2006/04/the_highs_and_lows_of_airline.html.
11. http://news.cheapflights.com/airlines/2005/10/jetblue_voted_t.html.
12. http://www.consumeraffairs.com/news04/2005/jetblue.html.
13. http://knowledge.wharton.upenn.edu/article/1342.cfm.

Chapter 6

1. http://www.bartleby.com/66/67/19467.html.
2. http://news.yahoo.com/s/ap/20060512/ap_on_hi_te/google_annual_meeting_2.
3. "The Seed of Apple's Innovation," *BusinessWeek.com* (October 12, 2004).
4. http://ei.cs.vt.edu/~history/Jobs.html.
5. http://video.google.com/videoplay?docid=-3168733759916419298.
6. http://www.lyricsxp.com/lyrics/i/is_that_all_there_is_peggy_lee.html.
7. http://promomagazine.com/entertainmentmarketing/starbucks_lionsgate_deal_011706.
8. http://www.imdb.com/title/tt0437800.
9. http://seattletimes.nwsource.com/html/businesstechnology/2002977465_denson07.html.

10. Dr. Mark Moon and John T. Mentzer, *Sales Forecasting Management: A Demand Management Approach* (Thousand Oaks, CA: Sage, 2004), http://bus.utk.edu/ivc/forecasting/articles/What%20Is%20World%20Class%20Forecasting.pdf.

11. See note 10.

12. http://www.inc.com/magazine/19990701/811.html.

13. http://earlystagevc.typepad.com/earlystagevc/2006/04/what_are_your_b.html.

14. http://www.pfdf.org/leaderbooks/L2L/spring97/kelleher.html.

15. Bill Nissim, "The ABCs of Great Brands," *Brandchannel.com* (September 30, 2005).

16. David Koenig (Associated Press), "Southwest Airlines Posts 54% Profit Increase," *TheWashingtonPost.com* (January 19, 2006).

17. http://www.southwest.com/about_swa/airborne.html.

18. http://www.coldwatercreek.com/asp/AboutCreek.asp.

19. http://www.businessweek.com/magazine/content/05_50/b3963124.htm.

20. http://finance.yahoo.com/q/bc?s=CWTR.

21. http://www.coldwatercreek.com/asp/AboutCreek.asp.

22. http://www.cioinsight.com/article2/0,1397,1875176,00.asp.

23. http://www.businessweek.com/magazine/content/05_19/b3932105_mz057.

24. http://www.coldwatercreek.com/asp/AboutCreek.asp.

25. http://finance.yahoo.com/q/co?s=CWTR.

26. http://www.coldwatercreek.com/asp/AboutCreek.asp.

27. http://www.cioinsight.com/article2/0,1397,1875176,00.asp\.

28. http://www.businessweek.com/magazine/content/05_50/b3963124.htm?campaign_id=search.

29. http://www.businessweek.com/magazine/content/05_23/b3936401.htm.

30. http://www.businessweek.com/magazine/content/05_50/b3963124.htm.

Chapter 7

1. Philip Kotler, *Marketing Management: Analysis, Planning, and Control*, 8th ed. (Engelwood Cliffs, NJ: Prentice Hall, 1993).

2. Sam Hill I, Jack McGrath, and Sandeep Dayal, "How to Brand Sand," *Strategy and Business* (Second Quarter 1998).

3. Harry Totonis and Chris Acito, "Branding the Bank: The Next Source of Competitive Advantage," *Insights Series* (1998).
4. Akio Morita, Edwin M. Reingold, and Mitsuko Shimomura, *Made in Japan: Akio Morita and the Sony Corporation* (New York: Dutton, 1986).
5. http://www.ogilvy.co.jp/english/o_mather_japan/emotional.
6. http://newsblaze.com/story/2006051706030100016.mwir/newsblaze/RESTAURA/Restaurants.html.
7. http://www.harbus.org/media/storage/paper343/news/2006/01/23/News/ChickFilAs.Secret.Spice.Marketing.Branding.And.Corporate.Values-1493844.shtml?norewrite200605061310&sourcedomain=www.harbus.org.
8. Scott Bedbury, *A New Brand World: Eight Principles for Achieving Brand Leadership in the Twenty-First Century* (New Tork: Penguin, 2003).
9. http://www.nyreport.com/index.cfm?fuseaction=Feature.showFeature&FeatureID=237&noheader=1.
10. http://www.biz-community.com/Article/196/82/9865.html.
11. http://www.boozallen.com/home/publications/article/659562?lpid=981162.
12. Interview, September 2003.
13. http://www.nike.com/ap/presto/language_select.html.
14. http://www.simonsays.com/content/book.cfm?tab=1&pid=405234.
15. http://groups.haas.berkeley.edu/marketing/PAPERS/AAKER/BOOKS/BUILDING/brand_personality.html.
16. http://www.appleinsider.com/article.php?id=1759.
17. http://www.cnn.com/2004/TECH/07/19/spain.zara/index.html.
18. http://money.cnn.com/magazines/fortune/fortune_archive/2000/09/04/286833/index.htm.
19. http://money.cnn.com/magazines/fortune/fortune_archive/2000/09/04/286833/index.htm.
20. http://www.businessweek.com/magazine/content/06_17/c3981003.htm.
21. http://www.inditex.com/en/who_we_are/our_team.
22. http://www.businessweek.com/magazine/content/06_17/c3981003.htm.
23. http://www.inditex.com/en/downloads/Press_Dossier_05.pdf—Similar pages.
24. http://www.icmr.icfai.org/casestudies/catalogue/Marketing1/MKTA023.htm.

Chapter 8

1. *Fortune* (September 23, 1991).
2. http://www.simonsays.com/content/book.cfm?tab=1&pid=407704.
3. http://panasonic.net/history/founder/chapter2/story2–06.html.
4. http://www.fortunepoint.com/quote.html.
5. http://www.questia.com/PM.qst?a=o&d=5001896228.
6. http://www.creatingcustomerevangelists.com/resources/evangelists /herb_kelleher.asp.
7. http://www.highbeam.com/library/docfree.asp?DOCID=1G1 :55427052&ctrlInfo=Round20%3AMode20a%3ADocG %3AResult&ao=.
8. William Meyers, "Conscience in a Cup of Coffee," *U.S.NEWS .com* (October 31, 2005).
9. http://www.businessweek.com/smallbiz/content/may2006/sb20060505 _893499.htm?link_position=link1.
10. http://fedex.com/us/about/news/speeches/postwareconomy.html.
11. http://seattlepi.nwsource.com/business/218261_starbucks31.html.
12. http://www.pb.com/cgi-bin/pb.dll/jsp/PressRoomSP.do ?ChannelName=/Our%20Company/Press%20Room /Speeches%20and%20Presentations&rootChannelName= /Our%20Company/Press%20Room&lang=en&country=U.S.
13. http://www.searchguild.com/googleblog.
14. http://www.kottke.org/plus/misc/google-playboy.html.
15. http://en.thinkexist.com/quotation/the_very_essence_of_leadership _is-that-you_have_a/225825.html.
16. For more information, contact BP p.l.c., 1 St James's Square, London SW1Y 4PD.
17. http://www.harpercollins.com/global_scripts/product_catalog/book _xml.asp?isbn=0060523808.
18. http://www.cfo.com/article.cfm/6874823/c_6880743?f=magazine _alsoinside.
19. http://www.cio.com/archive/031505/leadership.html.
20. http://news.iabc.com/index.php?s=press_releases&item=19.
21. http://www.management-issues.com/display_page.asp?section =research&id=1599.
22. http://www.cio.com/archive/031505/leadership.html.
23. http://www.irobot.com/sp.cfm?pageid=74.
24. http://www.irobot.com/sp.cfm?pageid=163.

25. http://pf.inc.com/magazine/20030701/25642.html.

26. http://www.businessweek.com/magazine/content/03_40/b3852129 _mz022.htm?campaign_id=search.

27. http://www.irobot.com/sp.cfm?pageid=203.

28. http://www.irobot.com/sp.cfm?pageid=42.

29. http://magazines.ivillage.com/goodhousekeeping/consumer /gbawards/photo/0,,680828_680829,00.html.

30. http://www.smartmoney.com/onedaywonder/index.cfm?story =20060503.

31. http://www.businessweek.com/technology/content/may2004 /tc2004056_2199_PG2_tc_168.htm.

Chapter 9

1. http://www.cdc.gov/niosh/stresswk.html.

2. http://www.salary.com/docs/resources/Salarycom_2005_Job _Satisfaction_Survey.pdf.

3. http://www.sowhatwhocareswhyyou.com/2006/06/the_downward_sp .html.

4. http://www.sinomedia.net/eurobiz/v200602/management0602 .html.

5. http://www.bloomberg.com/apps/news?pid=10000103&sid =a2oiXRjx9Gd4&refer=us.

6. http://www.greatachievements.org/?id=3878.

7. http://www.bloomberg.com/apps/news?pid=10000103&sid =a2oiXRjx9Gd4&refer=us.

8. http://www.greatachievements.org/?id=3878.

9. http://www.charlierose.com.

10. http://www.businessweek.com/magazine/content/06_10 /b3974001.htm.

11. http://www.randomhouse.com/crown/business/catalog/display .pperl?isbn=9780609608395.

12. Ram Charan, "Preface," *What the CEO Wants You to Know* (New York: Crown, 2001).

13. http://www.cmmol.net/sir_john_harvey_jones.htm.

14. http://www.wm.com/WM/ThinkGreen/heroes.asp.

15. See note 14.

16. Lyman K. Steil and Richard K. Bommelje, *Listening Leaders: The Ten Golden Rules to Listen, Lead & Succeed* (Edina, MN: Beaver's Pond Press, 2004), p. 25.
17. See note 16, p. 27.
18. http://www.businessweek.com/magazine/content/06_18/b3982075.htm.
19. See note 16, p. 149.
20. http://www.getoutaz.com/story/44?PHPSESSID =64f37192e10d72c458f316536aca68eb.
21. http://www.smartmoney.com/barrons/index.cfm?story=20060223.
22. http://www.texasroadhouse.com/content.php?menu=aboutus &display=n-guests.
23. http://www.smartmoney.com/barrons/index.cfm?story=20060223.
24. See note 23.

Chapter 10

1. http://rinkworks.com/said/yogiberra.shtml.
2. http://www.blakjak.demon.co.uk/gex_dtrs.htm.
3. http://www.marketingprofs.com/6/stroll109.asp.
4. http://www.umg.com.ua/download/Kiev.Business.5.19.06.ppt.
5. http://www.time.com/time/nation/article/0,8599,1206564,00.html.
6. http://www.brainyquote.com/quotes/authors/v/vince_lombardi.html.

Bibliography

Bedbury, Scott. *A New Brand World: Eight Principles for Achieving Brand Leadership in the Twenty-First Century.* New York: Penguin, 2003.

Bosworth, Michael, and John Holland. *CustomerCentric Selling.* New York: McGraw-Hill, 2003.

Charan, Ram. *What the CEO Wants You to Know: How Your Company Really Works.* New York: Crown, 2001.

Collins, Jim. *Good to Great: Why Some Companies Make the Leap . . . and Others Don't.* New York: HarperCollins, 2001.

Cox, Richard H. *Sports Psychology: Concepts and Applications*, 6th ed. New York: McGraw-Hill, 2006.

Curtis, David. "Building a Brand That Will Build Your Business," *New York Enterprise Report* (May 10, 2005), http://www.nyreport.com/index.cfm?fuseaction=Feature.showFeature&FeatureID=237.

Denove, Chris, and James Power. *Satisfaction: How Every Great Company Listens to the Voice of the Customer.* New York: Penguin, 2006.

Farzad, Roben, and Ben Elgin. "Googling for Gold." *BusinessWeek* (December 5, 2005), http://www.businessweek.com/magazine/content/05_49/b3962001.htm.

Friedman, Tom. *The World Is Flat: A Brief History of the Twenty-First Century.* New York: Farrar, Straus and Giroux, 2005.

Gallwey, Tim. *The Inner Game of Tennis.* New York: Random House, 1997.

Gerstner, Lou. *Who Says Elephants Can't Dance?* New York: HarperCollins, 2002.

Harvey-Jones, John. *Making It Happen.* London: HarperCollins Business, 2003.

Bibliography

Hill, Sam, Jack McGrath, and Sandeep Dayal. "How to Brand Sand." *Strategy and Business* (Second Quarter, 1998), http://www.strategy-business.com/press/16635507/16333.

Kim, W. Chan, and Renée Mauborgne. *Blue Ocean Strategy.* Boston, MA: Harvard Business School Publishing, 2005.

Kotler, Philip. *Marketing Management: Analysis, Planning, Implementation, and Control*, 8th ed. Englewood Cliffs, NJ: Prentice-Hall, 1993.

Kotter, John. *Matsushita Leadership.* New York: Free Press, 1997.

Moon, Mark, and John T. Mentzer. *Sales Forecasting Management: A Demand Management Approach.* Beverly Hills, CA: Sage, 2004.

Morita, Akio, Edwin M. Reingold, and Mitsuko Shimomura. *Made in Japan: Akio Morita and the Sony Corporation.* New York: Dutton, 1986.

Murphy, Shane. *The Sport Psych Handbook.* Champaign, IL: Human Kinetics, 2005.

Nissim, Bill. "The ABCs of Great Brands." http://www.brandchannel.com/papers_review.asp?sp_id=794 (accessed on September 30, 2005).

Peters, Tom, and Bob Waterman. *In Search of Excellence: Lessons from America's Best Run Companies.* New York: Warner Books, 1982.

Schultz, Howard. *Pour Your Heart into It: How Starbucks Built a Company One Cup at a Time.* New York: Hyperion, 1997.

Steil, Lyman, and Richard Bommelje. *Listening Leaders: The Ten Golden Rules to Listen, Lead & Succeed.* Edina, MN: Beaver's Pond Press, 2004.

Whiteley, Richard. *The Customer Driven Company.* Oxford, England: Perseus Books, 1993.

Yankelovich, Daniel, and David Meer. "Rediscovering Market Segmentation," *Harvard Business Review* (February 1, 2006).

Zyman, Sergio. *The End of Marketing as We Know It.* New York: HarperCollins, 1999.

Index

Index

Index